101 Top iPad Apps for Kids: Educational & Fun

By Mitchell Cogert, CEO

A Smart Friend, LLC

©2012 All rights reserved

ISBN: 146999447x

Acknowledgements

Thanks to everyone who helped to make this book a reality.

Thanks to my sister Val for her advice as a parent and teacher for over 10 years.

&

Shout-out to

Sandy (11 years old), Paige (9 years old), Malia (6 years old),

Brennan (4 years old) and Ellie (2 years old)

Table of Contents

KINDERGARTEN-ELEMENTARY: 5 TO 10 YEARS OLD

Introduction

App developers have designed remarkable iPad apps for kids that are educational and fun. The challenge is trying to find them among the thousands and thousands of apps in the iTunes store.

From a personal standpoint, the effort is very time consuming and risky. No matter what is written about an app, I know the developers are trying to sell me. At times, I would find a super app but other times the app did not live up to the hype. I would delete it.

I developed *101 Top iPad Apps for Kids: Educational and Fun* because I want to help you find the top iPad apps that are educational and fun for your child, and at the same time, group the apps in a meaningful way for your child's growth.

The age groups are toddler (under 3 years old), preschool (3-4 years old), kindergarten (5-6 years old), and elementary (7-10 years old).

And, to make them more meaningful, they are divided into educational areas, including Language & Literacy, Math, Creative Arts, and Intellectual Reasoning. Of course, there are other areas inside that are specific to a child's age such as telling time, hand-eye coordination and self-expression.

In *101 Top iPad Apps for Kids: Educational and Fun*, you will read in-depth reviews that cover what the app is, how it works, what it teaches, and its strengths and weaknesses. And, now, you'll be able to quickly determine which apps are best suited for your child based on age and educational needs.

The good news is that 78 of the top apps are compatible with the iPhone.

There are so many developers that have designed amazing apps for kids. They deserve to be praised because they are turning learning into a fun activity for kids. In the next section, I list and thank the developers whose apps were selected for this book.

Best wishes,

Mitchell Cogert

App Developers

Congratulations to the App Developers whose apps have been selected as the Top Educational and Fun Apps For Kids:

8Interactive Limited	www.8interactive.com/
22Learn, LLC	www.22learn.com/
24x7digital LLC	www.24x7digital.com/
ABCya.com	www.abcya.com
App-Zoo	
ArtelPlus	artelplus.com/
BFTV, LLC	www.babyfirsttv.com/
Blockdot, Inc.	www.blackdot.com
BrainPOP	www.brainpop.com/appst/landing/
CFC s.r.o.	www.22learn.com/
Cognitive Kid, Inc.	www.anselandclair.com/
Deepak Demiwal	www.demansol.com/index.html
Disney	www.disneybookapps.com
DJ International	
eFlashApps	www.eflashapps.com/
Fresh Factory	alfaproduction.com/
gdiplus	www.ptgdi.com/gdiplus/Home.html
Genera Kids	www.generainteractive.com/apps/
GO2STAT LLC	dl.dropbox.com/u/8499587/itubelist/index.html
Grasshopper Apps	www.GrasshopperApps.com/
i4software	www.i4software.com/products/
Idealix, Inc.	www.idealix.com

Innovative Mobile Apps	www.alligatorapps.com
ISBX	www.isbx.com/cowboys-and-aliens-the-kids/
Joy Preschool game	
Kids Place	KidsBestPlace.com/
Kids Games Club	KidsGamesClubHouse.com/
Launchpad Toys	launchpadtoys.com/
L'Escapadou	lescapadou.com
Learning Touch	learningtouch.com/products
Little Bee Speech	littlebeespeech.com/
Little Bit Studio	littlebitstudio.com/bugsandbuttons/
Little Potato Software	www.littlepotatosoftware.com/abfree.html
Loud Crow Interactive Inc.	www.loudcrow.com/
Alexandre Minard	ar-entertainment.net/learning/ipad.html
Mobile Education Tools	mobile-educationstore.com/
Motion Math	motionmathgames.com
National Geographic Society	www.nationalgeographic.com/community/email/
Nickelodeon	nickjr.com/
Newness World	newnessworld.com/
Oceanhouse Media	www.oceanhousemedia.com/
Open Solutions	www.babykidszone.com/games/
Pacific Spirit Media	www.pacificspiritmedia.com/
PBS Kids	pbskids.org/
David Ross Software	www.ross-soft.com/products/whimsy/
Dan Russell-Pinson	dan-russell-pinson.com
Sesame Street	www.callaway.com & www.familiesnearandfar.org

Shape Minds and Moving Images GmbH   shape-minds.com

Shoe the Goose   www.shoethegoose.com/

Siro Barbera Abril S.L.   www.sbainformatica.com/

Sergey Vasiliev   cloudgears.com/pictorial

Spinlight Studio   www.spinlight.com/apps/

Stepworks   www.kidztory.com

Summit Applications Corporation

Synthego   www.synthego.com/

TabTale LTD   www.tabtale.com/

Teknowledge Software

THUP   gamesmonkeypreschool.com/math.php

Tipitap Inc.   www.tipitap.com/

Toddler Teasers   www.toddlerteasers.com/

UmaChaka Media, Inc   tjandpals.com/

Zephyr Games   www.mathevolve.com/

Toddler-Preschool: 4 years old and under

Language & Literacy

Teaches kids letters, numbers, shapes and colors.

ABC Alphabet Phonics—Preschool Kids Game Free Lite

Recommended Age Group: Toddler-Preschool

Grades:

- Educational—B+

- Fun—B

- Overall—B+

Price: Free (No paid version)

Developer: GrasshopperApps.com

Compatible: iPhone

Review

What it is:

"ABC Alphabet Phonics—Preschool Kids Game Free Lite" is an educational app for preschoolers that uses colorful, appealing graphics to help kids identify letters of the alphabet by sight, touch and sound. It's a simple app that even babies as early as 9 months of age can enjoy.

How it Works:

The main menu is simple, with just a "play" button to start. A full-screen, white background comes up with graphics of the letters of the alphabet (anywhere between 1 and 10 depending on the setting). A voiceover instructs to "touch the A" for example. When the correct letter is touched, a red circle pops up around it and the voiceover gives an encouraging remark, such as "perfect!" If the wrong answer is touched, then a sound effect signals to try again. After successfully completing a page, a new page comes up with a different set of letters and the same instructions as before.

As the child progresses through the letters, more choices are given each time (up to a maximum of 10 letters). Many elements of this app are customizable. Parents can choose to include a display hint, which shows the letter at the top of the screen. This is good reinforcement for learning letters by both sight and sound.

There are also settings that allow parents to choose the minimum and maximum number of letters to display on the screen (between 1 and 10 for both). There is an option to delete any of the items as well as upload new ones. Finally, there is an option to record additional sounds. These could include success and error sounds as well as someone such as a parent recording saying the letters.

Part of the settings menu includes a library of letter graphics. There are six different choices, including upper and lowercase, which display large, colorful letters, letters with animal characters, letters with kid characters, letters with monkeys, and letters with colorful sketches. One or more of these can be used as options for the activity.

What it Teaches/Develops:

This app teaches very young children to identify letters of the alphabet through repetition and be able to recognize both upper and lowercase letters. It teaches using visual and verbal cues and provides positive feedback when successful.

The Good:

The app uses bright, colorful graphics, and the variation of characters is fun and will appeal to young children. It is incredibly easy to navigate and the instructions are simple so that even babies can successfully play this activity. The customizable settings are good so that parents can adjust the levels according to age, and the recordable options for sounds and uploading unique photos is a great feature that makes this app unique.

The Bad:

While the variety of letter graphics makes the app appealing, it can also make the activity confusing. If there are letters from all six libraries on the screen at one time, the difference in letter sizes, fonts and characters may actually make it harder for preschoolers to find the correct answer.

The word "phonics" is in the title of this app, but the concept is never introduced. The app would actually benefit from having the voiceover give the letter sound in addition to just identifying the letter.

Additional:

If parents choose letter graphics from only one or two of the libraries at a time, then this app will be a good, educational activity for preschoolers. The graphics are fun and bright, the navigation is simple, and kids will enjoy the photo touch concept.

AlphaBaby FREE

Recommended Age Group: Toddler-Preschool

Grades:

- Educational—A-
- Fun—A-
- Overall—A-

Price: Free (Full version $0.99)

Developer: Little Potato Software

Compatible: iPhone

Review

What it is:

"AlphaBaby Free" is a very simple app that lets small children explore the world of letters, numbers and shapes at their own pace and in their own way. By tapping, touching and pinching, toddlers can see letters pop up on the screen, shapes twirl in circles and numbers literally get bigger and smaller.

How it Works:

The app starts up immediately with a blank, white full screen. Tap anywhere on the screen and one of five types of items comes up: letters, numbers, shapes, pictures and colors. For example, a large, yellow number "9" might appear, or a bright purple "circle." A voiceover says the name of that item. Touch another area of the white screen and a new item pops up. The previous item remains as well.

Once an item is on the screen, kids can manipulate them. They can simply drag and move them to a new position, they can swipe to make them bounce around the screen, they can rotate the images with their fingers and they can pinch them to make them larger and smaller.

There are customizable options on the settings menu. Parents can choose between 1 and 20 items to have on the screen at a time (Once the maximum number of items is reached, the next time the screen is touched one of the previous items is no longer there). Parents can also choose one or more of the five types of items mentioned above.

Additionally, parents can customize the app to include their own photos and even

11

record their own voices, or their kids' voices, saying the names of the letters, shapes, numbers and colors.

What it Teaches/Develops:

Through repetition, this app teaches small children letter, shape, number and color recognition. Each time they interact with one of the items it reinforces the name of that item through sight, touch and sound. It also helps them begin to learn how to classify each into their own category.

The Good:

The app is so simple that even very young children can easily enjoy it. They will have fun manipulating the items and can even be creative in what they do with them, such as layering them on top of each other, shrinking and growing them and placing them where they want on the screen. The customized settings are a nice feature, especially recording familiar voices and uploading personal photos.

The Bad:

Other than the voiceover saying the name of each item, there are no other sound effects. There is no background music or fun sounds when kids move the items around on the screen. Including more sound would really enhance the experience of this app.

Navigating to the settings menu is not easy. Parents must press and hold the upper left corner of the screen, but it can take several tries to get it to come up.

In this free version there are a limited number of sounds and photos that can be added to the customized section. However, it doesn't take away anything from the app.

Additional:

Small children will really enjoy this app because of the fun ways they can manipulate the items on the screen. It's a simple but neat concept that will engage and interest toddlers, and the educational aspect is a good element as well.

Baby Hear & Read Nouns Lite

Recommended Age Group: Toddler-Preschool

Grades:

- Educational—B+

- Fun—B+

- Overall—B+

Price: Free (Full version $0.99)

Developer: Open Solutions

Compatible: iPhone

Review

What it is:

Teaching kids basic nouns is an important concept, and "Baby Hear & Read Nouns Lite--See, Listen and Spell with 3D Animals" is an app that aims to do that. Using humorous animal characters, kids can learn a variety of words and how to spell them with the touch of a finger.

How it Works:

The app forgoes a traditional start up menu, and instead opens directly to a screen with thumbnails of all the animal graphics. There are nine on the first page, then swipe to see another set of nine. Touch an animal to bring up a full screen version.

For example, a pink pig character is holding a giant pencil. A voiceover says the word "pencil," then spells out the word one letter at a time. Each letter is highlighted in red as it is spelled. When finished, the screen returns to the thumbnail menu.

There is a setting to have the app play in slideshow mode, which would automatically advance to the next graphic and word. Additional settings include turning the text, voiceover and spelling voice on or off. There's also an option to have either four or nine thumbnails to a page.

What it Teaches/Develops:

This app teaches children the correct names for a variety of nouns. It helps them learn the pronunciation for each word and for older children, it teaches them how to spell it as well.

The Good:

This app is extremely easy for very young children to navigate. They don't even need to press a play button to start or to return to the main menu. The animal characters are creative, funny and entertaining.

The Bad:

There is no animation with this app. The graphics don't move or make any sound. The voiceover is rather monotone and doesn't provide much enthusiasm. The app is supposed to teach children nouns, but there is no explanation to help them understand the definition of a noun. There is a version of this app for $0.99 that includes more than 100 words.

Additional:

Graphically, this app is very original and looks appealing to any preschooler. The concept of teaching nouns is good, and with additional animation or sound the app would be more dynamic and enhance the experience.

Baby Hear & Read Verbs Lite

Recommended Age Group: Toddler-Preschool

Grades:

- Educational—B+

- Fun—B+

- Overall—B+

Price: Free (Full version $0.99)

Developer: Open Solutions

Compatible: iPhone

Review

What it is:

In "Baby Hear & Read Verbs Lite--See, Listen and Spell with 3D Animals" the creative, funny animal characters are back, only this time they're helping kids learn to say and spell words that are verbs.

How it Works:

Rather than a traditional start up menu, the app opens directly to a screen with thumbnails of all the animal graphics. There are nine on the first page, then swipe to see another set of nine. Touch an animal to bring up a full screen version.

For example, there is a graphic of a dog lifting weights. A voiceover says the word "exercise," then spells out the word one letter at a time. Each letter is highlighted in red as it is spelled. When finished, the screen returns to the thumbnail menu.

There is a setting to have the app play in slideshow mode, which would automatically advance to the next graphic and word. Additional settings include turning the text, voiceover and spelling voice on or off. There's also an option to have either four or nine thumbnails to a page.

What it Teaches/Develops:

This app teaches children the correct names for a variety of verbs. It helps them learn the pronunciation for each word and for older children, it teaches them how to spell it as well.

The Good:

This app is extremely easy for very young children to navigate. They don't even need to press a play button to start or to return to the main menu. The animal characters are creative, funny and entertaining.

The Bad:

Similar to "Baby Hear & Read Nouns Lite," there is no animation with this app. The graphics don't move or make any sound. The voiceover is flat and resembles a computerized voice. There is a version of this app for $0.99 that includes more than 80 words.

Additional:

These apps have so much to offer graphically and could really entertain kids. The concept is important and learning to spell words by sight and sound is good. With additional animation or sound, the app would be more dynamic and enhance the experience.

If You're Happy and You Know It

Recommended Age Group: Toddler-Preschool

Grades:

- Educational—B+

- Fun—B+

- Overall—B+

Price: Free (In-app purchases starting at $0.99)

Developer: Kids Games Club

Compatible: iPhone

Review

What it is:

For simple games and a fun sing-along song, "If You're Happy and You Know It" is an app that toddlers will enjoy and find a number of activities to keep them busy that they can navigate on their own.

How it Works:

From the main menu there are two options, "Play" and "Games." Touch "Play" and a colorful screen comes up with two characters dancing to the familiar song "If You're Happy and You Know it." The music plays in the background and a voiceover sings the song. The words to the song show up at the top of the screen, and the characters clap during the song.

Under the "Games" menu option there are three activities: "The Animal Train," "The Magical Animal Kingdom," and "Animal Puzzles." In "The Animal Train" a bright train graphic chugs across the screen stopping to spell out each animal as it passes. In "The Magical Animal Kingdom" different animals tell a story and kids use the "magic wand" to color in the picture that goes along with the story. In "Animal Puzzles" kids drag simple puzzle pieces to the correct positions to create a picture of an animal.

What it Teaches/Develops:

This app encourages children to participate in an interactive sing-along song, complete with teaching them lyrics and actions. The games included with the app focus on teaching names of animals and how to spell them, along with word recognition.

The Good:

This app offers a variety of fun, simple activities that kids of this age would really enjoy. The combination of a song, stories, coloring, puzzles and learning letters is a great way to keep young children entertained. All of the activities are easy to navigate and appealing to kids.

The Bad:

The interactive song in this free version only includes the first part to "If You're Happy and You Know it Clap Your Hands." The song continues on the screen with the next verse, but a large ad covers up most of the screen and in order to see the graphics in the background, the full version must be purchased. This also occurs during the games.

Additional:

This is a cute app for toddlers, but the free version is rather limited. Individual activities can be purchased for $0.99 each, or the full version is available for $1.99, which includes the full song pack, a peek-a-boo game, a math game pack and coloring pages.

Letters Toddler Preschool

Recommended Age Group: Toddler-Preschool

Grades:

- Educational--A-

- Fun—B

- Overall—B+

Price: $0.99 (No free version. Additional in-app products at $0.99 each.)

Developer: Toddler Teasers

Compatible: iPhone

Review

What it is:

For parents who want to teach their toddler letter recognition, "Letters Toddler Preschool" is a kid-friendly app that children will enjoy. With simple activities to choose from and a fun reward system, young kids will be able to easily navigate this learning tool on their own.

How it Works:

The main menu gives three options for play: "quizzing," "flash cards" and "toy box" game modes. For quizzing, a set of brightly colored letters appears on the screen across a colored background. A voiceover asks to "find the letter A" for example. Touch the letter "A", and either cheering or clapping is heard. After several rounds, a virtual "sticker" is awarded. Kids touch the sticker they want and then to get place it on a colorful picnic background. The voiceover also says the name of the item on the sticker.

For the flash card game, a full-screen card appears with a brightly colored letter in the middle. The voiceover says the letter. Swipe the page, and a new flash card with a different letter comes up.

The toy box mode has a number of consecutive activities. The first is a "balloon pop." Touch the colored balloons on screen and they each "pop" to reveal a different letter. That particular set of letters then go to the "circus" where they become colorful cannonballs. Drag and load one into the cannon and watch it shoot out. Next the set of letters go to the railroad where kids can attach them like train cars behind an engine. The letter train chugs along the track as the voiceover announces each one. Finally the set of letters become building blocks that kids can drag and "stack" on top of each other. Once finished, the set of activities starts over with the balloon pop game revealing a new set of letters.

What it Teaches/Develops:

For young children this app teaches them letter recognition through repetition. The fact that each activity in one round of the toy box game uses the same set of letters is a good way to reinforce what kids are learning.

The Good:

This is a simple app that's easy for small children to navigate on their own. The bright colors, animation and music make for a nice experience. The "clapping and cheering" during the quizzing mode will really please toddlers and give them positive encouragement. The sticker reward system is also a great tool, and there is a setting option that enables the sticker page to be saved even after exiting the game.

The Bad:

In this version of the app there is only one category available, so it really limits variety in the activities. The letter flash cards won't keep a toddler's attention for long. The sticker rewards are only offered with the quizzing game, and while additional sticker page "backgrounds" are available, they must be purchased separately.

The Ugly:

This $0.99 version only comes with one category: letters. Other categories are available as individual in-app purchases, or there is a complete version that comes with 30 different categories.

Additional:

This app is a good supplement to have with other teaching tools. It provides some interest and variety, and kids will have fun with the different activities and sticker page. However, in order to take full advantage of everything this app has to offer, additional categories need to be purchased.

Simon Says - Classic All in One Vocal Memory Game

Recommended Age Group: Toddler-Preschool

Grades:

- Educational--B

- Fun—A-

- Overall—B+

Price: Free (Full version $1.99)

Developer: Kids Place

Compatible: iPhone

Review

What it is:

"Simon Says-Classic All in One Vocal Memory Game" builds on the classic Simon Says game by challenging their memories in a variety of categories using a fun, colorful interface.

How it Works:

This app features two games, both accessible from the main menu. Touch the "smiley face" for sounds and colors and touch the "paint palette" for a voiceover and colors. In the sounds and colors game a screen comes up with different colored squares. The app highlights them in a certain order, accompanied by sounds. Kids must touch the squares in the same order that was given.

The paint palette game is similar to the first game except a voiceover says the name of the color each time it's chosen. If the sequence is repeated correctly, your child is rewarded with positive feedback.

There are eight different Simon Says games. As kids continue to play, the app automatically increases the level of difficulty.

What it Teaches/Develops:

This app helps children practice their memory skills and it improves their concentration. For younger kids it also helps them learn colors through sight and sound.

The Good:

This app has colorful graphics and really challenges kids to focus and recall directions in the correct sequence. It's easy to navigate and provides a fun, dynamic experience for kids.

The Bad:

The app only works in the portrait mode, rather than horizontal like most apps do on the iPad.

Additional:

"Simon Says-Classic All in One Vocal Memory Game" is a great way to play an interactive version of Simon Says and challenge a kid's memory of patterns and sounds. There is also a full version for $1.99 that includes the alphabet, numbers and shapes.

Math

Teaches kids numbers and how to count.

Montessori Counting Board—Counting for Kids

Recommended Age Group: Toddler-Preschool

Grades:

- Educational—B+

- Fun—B

- Overall—B+

Price: Free (No paid version)

Developer: Grasshopper Apps

Compatible: iPhone

Review

What it is:

If you're looking for an app that will help your toddler learn how to count, then "Montessori Counting Board—Counting for Kids" is perfect. With just the touch of a finger, even the smallest hands can easily count the large, colorful squares on the screen.

How it Works:

The app opens onto a large, wooden, counting "board." The easiest level starts with three colored squares. Touch the first square and the number "1" pops up on the square inside a yellow circle. A voiceover says the number "one," and a square in a corresponding color is displayed along the bottom of the board. Touch another square and the number "2" pops up on it inside a green circle. A voiceover again says the number "two" and a second square is displayed along the bottom of the board. Now both squares along the bottom are green and the number "2" is next to them. No matter which square your child touches, it will count that as the next number. At this level, there is no "wrong" answer.

There are five different ways kids can count on the board. They can simply count by touch, as described above; they can count up in order; they can count down in order; they can drag the squares to the bottom of the board and count up as they do; or they can drag the squares to the bottom of the board and count down.

There is a settings tab that allows parents to customize the app. Not only can you choose which of the five ways to count, but you can also choose if the numbers appear progressively in order or at random. You can also choose how many items to start with (between 3 and 20) and the maximum number of items to display (again between 3 and 20).

What it Teaches/Develops:

This app teaches very young children how to count using sight, sound and touch. They will learn how to count from 0 to 20 and from 20 down to 0. They will also learn number recognition and counting objects, which is an important concept as they reach pre-school and kindergarten.

The Good:

With its large, colorful squares, clear, easily understood voiceover and simple interactive experience, even very small children will be successful at this app. There are plenty of prompts that serve as guides, and toddlers will enjoy having an app that they are able to play all by themselves.

The Bad:

Since the numbers don't go higher than 20, if your child already knows how to count that high, then this app won't offer much challenge or stimulation. Counting squares is simple, but that's all children will be doing. The shapes don't change, and there is no "reward" system for being successful.

Additional:

Once parents familiarize themselves with the settings, this app is a great aide in helping toddlers learn to count. With a variety of ways the app teaches counting, children will enjoy this quick, learning activity.

Numbers Toddler Preschool

Recommended Age Group: Toddler-Preschool

Grades:

- Educational—B

- Fun—B

- Overall—B

Price: $0.99 (No free version)

Developer: Toddler Teasers

Compatible: iPhone

Review

What it is:

For parents who want to teach their toddler number recognition, "Numbers Toddler Preschool" is a kid-friendly app that children will enjoy. With simple activities to choose from and a fun reward system, young kids will be able to easily navigate this learning tool on their own.

How it Works:

The main menu gives three options for play: "quizzing," "flash cards" and "toy box" game modes. For quizzing, a set of brightly colored numbers appears on the screen across a colored background. A voiceover asks to "find the number two" for example. Touch the number two, and either cheering or clapping is heard. After several rounds, a virtual "sticker" is awarded. Kids touch the sticker they want and then to get place it on a colorful picnic background. The voiceover also says the name of the item on the sticker.

For the flash card game, a full-screen card appears with a brightly colored number in the middle. The number is also spelled out underneath. The voiceover says the number. Swipe the page, and a new flash card with a different number (not necessarily in order) comes up.

The toy box mode has a number of consecutive activities. The first is a "balloon pop." Touch the colored balloons on screen and they each "pop" to reveal a different random number. That particular set of numbers then go to the "circus" where they become colorful cannonballs. Drag and load one into the cannon and watch it shoot out. Next the set of numbers go to the railroad where kids can attach them like train cars behind an engine. The number train chugs along the track as the voiceover announces each one. Finally the set of numbers become building blocks that kids can drag and "stack" on top of each other. Once finished, the set of activities starts over with the balloon pop game revealing a new set of numbers.

There are some customizable options with this app. Depending on the age of the child, parents can choose to use only the numbers 1-10, or expand it from numbers 1-99. There are also three language options: English, Spanish and French.

What it Teaches/Develops:

For young children this app teaches them number recognition through repetition. The fact that each activity in one round of the toy box game uses the same set of numbers is a good way to reinforce what kids are learning. In order to be successful at the activities, children must be able to know their numbers out of order since the numbers never occur in sequence, even in the flash card mode. And for children who already know their numbers through ten, it gives them an opportunity to practice with numbers up to 99.

The Good:

This is a simple app that's easy for small children to navigate on their own. The bright colors, animation and music make for a nice experience. The "clapping and cheering" during the quizzing mode will really please toddlers and give them positive encouragement. The sticker reward system is also a great tool, and there is a setting option that enables the sticker page to be saved even after exiting the game.

The Bad:

This app only teaches number recognition, not numbers in sequence or counting. And in this version of the app there is only one category available, so it really limits variety in the activities. The number flash cards won't keep a toddler's attention for long. The sticker rewards are only offered with the quizzing game, and while additional sticker page "backgrounds" are available, they much be purchased separately.

This $0.99 version only comes with one category: numbers. Other categories are available as individual in-app purchases, or there is a complete version that comes with 30 different categories.

Additional:

This app is a good supplement to have with other teaching tools. It provides some interest and variety, and kids will have fun with the different activities and sticker page. However, in order to take full advantage of everything this app has to offer, additional categories need to be purchased.

TallyTots

Recommended Age Group: Toddler-Preschool

Grades:

- Educational--A
- Fun—A-
- Overall—A

Price: $1.99 (No free version)

Developer: Spinlight Studio

Compatible: iPhone

Review

What it is:

To help younger children learn how to count up to the number 20, "Tally Tots" features a variety of fun, colorful activities tied to each number. Kids will love counting once they've had a chance to experience this app.

How it Works:

There are two different main activities for this app. The first is a sing-along numbers song accessed by the musical notes icon on the bottom right of the screen. A voiceover sings a number song with the visuals that represent the numbers from one to twenty, and kids are encouraged to sing along.

The second activity is a counting game. Select a number from one to twenty on the cards shown on the screen. A voiceover encourages kids to count along starting with number one and going up through the number selected.

Next, the voiceover introduces an activity by asking a question or making a statement. The corresponding activity appears, and kids must complete that activity as directed. The app lets kids know when they are finished, and they can pick another number from one to twenty.

What it Teaches/Develops:

This app teaches young children how to count from numbers one through twenty. Limiting kids to only these numbers helps to ensure they have them mastered, which is a necessary skill at this age.

The Good:

This app uses bright, colorful graphics and fun activities to teach kids how to count to twenty. The sing-along song is engaging and encourages kids to actively participate in the learning process. All of the activities are age appropriate and kids will enjoy playing along.

The Bad:

There is nothing bad about this app.

Additional:

"Tally Tots" is a simple, easy-to-use app that is focused on teaching young children one thing: how to count from one to twenty. It's a great educational tool to have available for kids to ensure their readiness prior to entering kindergarten.

Team Umizoomi Math: Zoom into Numbers HD

Recommended Age Group: Toddler-Preschool

Grades:

- Educational--A-
- Fun—A-
- Overall—A-

Price: $4.99 (No free version)

Developer: Nickelodeon

Compatible: Not with iPhone

Review

What it is:

Nickelodeon's Team Umizoomi app encourages preschool children to recognize numbers, the order of numbers, and how to add and subtract. This app has five fun, math related games that take place in Umi city. Kids can earn badges, trophies and even the key to the city.

How it Works:

There are five games in the app:

1. Toy Store Counting: This is a counting game where your child is directed to touch different toys. When your child touches the toy, an Umizoomi team member counts each toy.

2. Number Bubbles: This is a number identification game. A number is randomly selected when your child spins a wheel on a gumball machine. Next, bubbles appear on the screen with different number of objects inside each one. Your child must pop the bubbles with the number selected from the gumball machine.

3. Rolling Toy Parade: A number ordering game. This is where your child is told to drag items with numbers on them in the right sequence starting at the number 1.

4. Race Around Umi City: A number comparison game. Here, your child controls a car driving down a street. A team character announces a number to drive your car under. Two numbers appear your child must drive under the right number.

5. Up! Up! And Balloons! This is an addition and subtraction game using balloons. Math and subtraction problems are given with three possible answers.

Success in each one of these games earns your child a badge.

What it Teaches/Develops:

This app teaches kids numbers, their order and how to add and subtract.

The Good:

This app is very involving with the fun, interactive math games. The Umizoomi Team members provide direction and positive reinforcement. The games are colorful and the animation is excellent.

The Bad:

There is nothing bad about this app.

Additional:

Team Umizoomi Math: Zoom into Numbers HD is a very popular game among kids and parents. It is easy-to-use, covers key math concepts, and provides a positive learning experience.

Creative Arts

Promotes creativity through pretend play, song and coloring.

Elves Dress Up-costume party clothing game HD by TabTale

Recommended Age Group: Toddler-Preschool

Grades:

- Educational--B

- Fun—B

- Overall—B

Price: Free (No paid version)

Developer: TabTale LTD

Compatible: iPhone

Review

What it is:

"Elves Dress Up Costume Party clothing game" lets toddlers play dress up with two colorful, cute elves. They can add a variety of items to the elves, take them off, change the color of their clothes, and have lots of interactive fun.

How it Works:

The main screen displays two funny large-nosed, curly haired elves in their underwear with their hands raised overhead ready to be "dressed." Lying on the floor in front of each elf are items of clothing: shoes, socks, pants, shirt, cape and hat. To the left of the elves is a large button with a shirt inside. Stars in the shape of a heart sparkle around the elves.

Children interact with the elves simply by touching the screen. Tap on the elves to see them giggle and leap in the air. Tap on any individual item of clothing on the floor and it is automatically placed on the elf's body. Simply tap any item of clothing to remove it again.

To change the color of the clothing items, tap the shirt inside the large button. The colors change from red to blue to green.

For hints on where to tap, touch the hidden book at the bottom of the screen. A menu appears with a tips/light bulb icon. Select "tips" and blue hands flash on the screen to illustrate where to tap the screen.

What it Teaches/Develops:

This app helps to teach self-awareness and creativity as your child selects clothing items and colors to dress and undress the elves. It promotes pretend play as well, which is an important developmental stage at this age.

The Good:

The app is a fun, interactive, dress up game for toddlers. It uses happy elves, sparkling stars, and bright colors to capture children's attention. Both boys and girls will enjoy playing with these funny characters.

The Bad:

The app is a simple one with only two elves, three color choices, and a few items of clothing. Once a child has played it a few times, there isn't much left for them to explore.

Additional:

"Elves Dress Up-costume party clothing game" is a fun little app for toddlers. It also serves as a way for the developer to introduce parents to their line of interactive children's books, which kids would also enjoy.

Happy Earth Day, Dear Planet

Recommended Age Group: Toddler-Preschool

Grades:

- Educational--B
- Fun—B+
- Overall—B

Price: Free (No paid version)

Developer: TabTale LTD

Compatible: iPhone

Review

What it is:

Singing familiar songs is a fun activity for little ones, and "Happy Earth Day, Dear Planet-Interactive Sing Along Song" is a good example. This is a sing-along app that encourages toddlers to sing a cheerful song over and over again. A colorful screen adds animals and birds that respond to touch with limited sound and movement.

How it Works:

After touching "play" the app opens to a colorful scene with trees, grass, ducks, rabbits and more. A bold headline reads "Happy Earth Day To You." A voiceover over sings "Happy Earth Day To You," using in the familiar "Happy Birthday" tune. During the song, some of the graphics move on the screen.

When your child taps on any of the animals or trees in the scene, they react with a brief sound, like a quack from a duck, the humming from humming birds, or a "whee" from a rabbit. Tap any word in the headline "Happy Earth Day To You" to restart the song. Each word in the lyrics is highlighted as the voiceover sings.

To get tips on where to tap, touch the hidden book at the bottom of the screen. A menu appears with a tips/light bulb icon. Select tips and blue hands flash on the screen to illustrate where to tap the screen.

What it Teaches/Develops:

This app encourages young kids to sing along with a very simple song. The familiar tune is engaging and the highlighted words help reinforce what they are learning and promote word recognition.

The Good:

This is a colorful, cheerful musical app. The scene is bright and filled with friendly animals and birds. The "Happy Birthday" tune is memorable and easy for young children to sing along to.

The Bad:

The tips/light bulb button is helpful as it flashes many blue hands on screen to show where your child can tap the screen to get a duck to quack or a rabbit to say "whee." However, these blue hands disappear quickly.

Additional:

This is a fun, simple app that very young children, even babies, will enjoy. Kids at this age love repetition and will have fun hearing the song over and over again. The extra animation is a great way to keep kids engaged even after the song is finished playing.

Scratch a Sketch Lite

Recommended Age Group: Toddler-Preschool

Grades:

- Educational--B

- Fun—B

- Overall—B

Price: Free (Full version $0.99)

Developer: BFTV, LLC

Compatible: iPhone

Review

What it is:

Even the youngest child will be able to enjoy "Scratch a Sketch Lite," which is an app that lets children "color" simply by swiping the screen with their finger to reveal a colorful image hidden behind it.

How it Works:

To use the "Scratch a Sketch Lite," press "play" from the main menu. A completely black screen appears with the instructions "Place your finger on the screen."

Once kids place their finger on the screen the instructions disappear. When they lift their finger off the screen, only the area of the screen that was just touched reveals there is something underneath. As kids continue to rub the screen a colorful image is slowly uncovered.

When enough of the black is rubbed off and most of the image is revealed, the entire image is automatically shown. A voiceover provides positive feedback such as "good job" or "great."

This repeats three more times with a new image.

What it Teaches/Develops:

This app helps small children improve their hand-eye coordination. It also improves their fine motor skills, which is important for children who are too young to play some of the other more advanced art apps.

The Good:

This app encourages a child to use their fingers and interact with the screen. It is easy for even the youngest children to navigate and successfully play. The images are extremely colorful and bright, and the verbal positive feedback is good encouragement.

The Bad:

There are only four possible images that the screen reveals. If children want additional pictures, there is a full version available for $0.99 that offers more images.

Additional:

This is a very simple app that even babies can enjoy. They will have fun discovering what is hidden behind the screen—it's like an interactive form of peek-a-boo.

The Rabbit & The Turtle - Forest Race Game for Children

Recommended Age Group: Toddler-Preschool

Grades:

- Educational--B

- Fun—B

- Overall—B

Price: Free (Full version $1.99)

Developer: TabTale LTD

Compatible: iPhone

Review

What it is:

"The Rabbit & the Turtle - Forest Race" is an app that introduces small children to the classic story of "The Tortoise and the Hare." Kids are able to interact with the rabbit and the turtle during the race in a fun, animated environment.

How it Works:

The full screen scene features one page from the classic tortoise and hare tale. It illustrates the final stage of the race between a rabbit and a turtle. The turtle is in the lead, but the rabbit is close behind.

The scene is filled with onlookers. A few animals wave flags like cheering fans. A bird bobs up and down in the wind. A fox holds a starter's pistol. There's even a raccoon with a camera ready to snap a picture of the winner. Touch of any of these characters to see them animated.

To continue the race to the finish line, kids tap the turtle and the rabbit. The turtle always wins, and the crowd cheers when he moves past the finish line.

To get tips on where to tap the screen, touch the hidden book at the bottom of the screen. A menu appears with a tips/light bulb icon. Select tips and blue hands flash on the screen to illustrate where to tap.

What it Teaches/Develops:

This app is a way for young children to familiarize themselves with a classic story and learn through interaction. Parents can play the app with their child and talk about the lesson the story teaches.

The Good:

The illustrated scene is colorful and cheerful, and the animal characters will appeal to children. There are many opportunities for interaction and to see animated parts of the story, which is fun for kids at this age.

The Bad:

The tips/light bulb button is helpful as it flashes many blue hands on screen to show where your child can tap the screen to get interaction. However, these blue hands disappear quickly.

Additional:

"The Rabbit and the Turtle - Forest Race" is a fun, simple interactive app. This free version only provides one page from the story. However, there is a full version available for $1.99 that tells the complete story of The Tortoise and the Hare.

Intellectual Reasoning

Kids make sense of the world around them.

Animals Forest Adventure Game for Children

Recommended Age Group: Toddler-Preschool

Grades:

- Educational—B+

- Fun—B+

- Overall—B+

Price: Free (No paid version)

Developer: TabTale LTD

Compatible: iPhone

Review

What it is:

Using lots of animation and colorful graphics, "Animals Forest Adventure Game for Children" helps preschoolers learn the different animals found in a forest, what sounds they make and how to spell the words for those animals.

How it Works:

Touch "play" on the main menu and a screen full of animated animals in a bright, colorful forest setting come to life. Touch one of the animals, such as the "fox," and a voiceover says the name of the animal, the word pops up on the screen and the picture of the fox hops up and down.

There are a wide variety of animals in this app, including a squirrel, snake, parrot, hedgehog, fish, mouse, bird, cat, and chameleon. Some of the animals make sound effects when they move, and there are hidden surprises as well. For example, animals popping in and out of tree houses when tapped.

Even when the app is not in play, there is a lot of constant animation on the screen, as well as sound effects.

What it Teaches/Develops:

This app helps preschoolers learn about a variety of animals, the sounds they make and begin to recognize the words for each animal. The concept is reinforced through repetition as kids touch the animals repeatedly to see the fun animation and hear the sounds.

The Good:

The graphics in this app are very well done and resemble bright, appealing illustrations out of a children's picture book. The animation is also well done, and with all of the hidden surprises, kids will enjoy exploring the page to find many surprises. The variety of animals is nice, and it's a very professional, thought-out concept.

The Bad:

Unfortunately, there is only one activity page for this app. Once kids have experienced all of the animals and hidden objects a few times, there is nothing left to explore. If there were several different settings with additional animals, it would provide a much more dynamic and fulfilling experience.

Additional:

This is a high-quality app with many aspects that will appeal to preschoolers. It's also simple with easy navigation. Kids will have fun with it the first few times they play. The only downside is the lack of variety with the single activity.

Animal Parade Game from Noah's Ark

Recommended Age Group: Toddler-Preschool

Grades:

- Educational—B

- Fun—B

- Overall—B

Price: Free (Full version is Noah's Ark-An Interactive Children's Bible Tale $1.99)

Developer: TabTale LTD

Compatible: iPhone

Review

What it is:

Many kids are familiar with the story of Noah's Ark, and "Animal Parade Game from Noah's Ark" is a simple activity that helps toddlers learn about the animals that were on the ark.

How it Works:

After touching "play" a full screen image comes up of Noah standing beside his ark. Several animals are in line, two by two, waiting to get on the ark. Touch the first animal, a lion, and it moves onto the ark. It also gives a roaring sound effect. Touch the second lion, and Noah says the word "lion" and the word comes up on the screen. Repeat this for all the animals in line until everyone is aboard the ark.

What it Teaches/Develops:

This app teaches small children the names of different animals and the sounds they make. The animals include lions, giraffes, zebras, bears, monkeys, seals and even gazelles. If kids play more than once, then they will benefit from the repetition of hearing the animal names, their sounds, and even seeing the words for each animal.

The Good:

The graphics are very appealing and the concept of learning about animals by tying them into the story of Noah's Ark is very creative. The navigation is simple. Kids need only to touch each animal in order to hear it and watch it walk onto the ark. There is even extra animation. Touch the sky and it thunders, or touch Noah and he moves.

The Bad:

There are only about a dozen animals to help move onto the ark and then the activity is done. There aren't any additional activities with the app or extra levels where you can get more animals. Apparently, this app is just one activity from an accompanying app by the developer, "Noah's Ark—An Interactive Children's Bible Tale," but this is a separate purchase.

Additional:

The concept behind this app is good and the graphics are very well done. Kids will enjoy helping the animals onto Noah's Ark and exploring to find the hidden animation.

Animals Toddler Preschool

Recommended Age Group: Toddler-Preschool

Grades:

- Educational—B+

- Fun—B+

- Overall—B+

Price: $0.99 (No free version)

Developer: Toddler Teasers

Compatible: iPhone

Review

What it is:

For parents who want to teach their preschooler animal recognition, "Animals Toddler Preschool" is a kid-friendly app that children will enjoy. With simple activities to choose from and a fun reward system, young kids will be able to easily navigate this learning tool on their own.

How it Works:

The main menu gives three options for play: "quizzing," "flash cards" and "toy box" game modes. For quizzing, a set of animal graphics appears on the screen across a colored background. A voiceover asks to "find the bear" for example. Touch the bear, and either cheering or clapping is heard. After several rounds, a virtual "sticker" is awarded. Kids touch the sticker they want and then to get place it on a colorful picnic background. The voiceover also says the name of the item on the sticker.

For the flash card game, a full-screen card appears with a graphic of an animal in the middle. The word is also spelled out underneath. The voiceover says the name of the animal. Swipe the page, and a new flash card with a different animal comes up.

The toy box mode has a number of consecutive activities. The first is a "balloon pop." Touch the colored balloons on screen and they each "pop" to reveal a different animal. That set of animals then go to the "circus" where they become colorful cannonballs. Drag and load one into the cannon and watch it shoot out. Next the animals go to the railroad where kids can attach them like train cars behind an engine. The animal train chugs along the track as the voiceover announces each one. Finally the animals become building blocks that kids can drag and "stack" on top of each other. Once finished, the set of activities starts over with the balloon pop game revealing a new set of animals.

There are some customizable options with this app, including settings for rewards, saving the sticker page and choosing the voiceover to be in English, French or Spanish.

What it Teaches/Develops:

For young children this app teaches them animal recognition through repetition. The fact that each activity in one round of the toy box game uses the same set of animals is a good way to reinforce what kids are learning. There are 18 possible animals that can come up for each activity, which is a wide variety for kids to learn.

The Good:

This is a simple app that's easy for small children to navigate on their own. The bright colors, animation and music make for a nice experience. The "clapping and cheering" during the quizzing mode will really please toddlers and give them positive encouragement. The sticker reward system is also a great tool.

The Bad:

This app teaches animal recognition through pictures and words, but it doesn't explore animal sounds, which would be a nice addition. The animal graphics in the app are rather flat and not very dynamic. The sticker rewards are only offered with the quizzing game, and while additional sticker page "backgrounds" are available, they much be purchased separately.

This $0.99 version only comes with the animal category. Other categories are available as individual in-app purchases, or there is a complete version that comes with 30 different categories.

Additional:

This app is a good supplement to have with other teaching tools. It provides some interest and variety, and kids will have fun with the different activities and sticker page. However, in order to take full advantage of everything this app has to offer, additional categories need to be purchased.

Animals Zoo Interactive Flash Cards

Recommended Age Group: Toddler-Preschool

Grades:

- Educational—B

- Fun—B

- Overall—B

Price: Free (No paid version)

Developer: TabTale LTD

Compatible: iPhone

Review

What it is:

Apps that teach small children to recognize animals and their sounds are popular, and "Animals Zoo—Interactive Flash Cards--Jungle Wild Life Farm Pets Animal Sounds Kids Learning Game HD" is a good one to add to the list.

How it Works:

Touch "play" from the main menu to bring up the first "flash card." A full screen graphical background comes up with an illustration an animal, such as "horse." The word is displayed in large, colorful text across the top of the screen. Touch the word and a voiceover says "horse." Touch the picture of the horse and it moves then "neighs." Soft music plays in the background the entire time. Touch the forward arrow in the upper right corner of the screen to advance to the next flash card.

There are 40 different animal flash cards with this app, all from a number of categories including jungle wildlife, farm and sea animals, pets, birds and endangered species. Each animal has its own special animation and all of the flash cards have a consistent, illustrated look. On the settings menu there is an option to scroll through all of the animal pages, and there is even an option to email any of the animal pages to someone else.

What it Teaches/Develops:

This app teaches kids animal recognition, the sounds they make and the words that go with them. Using repetition and consistency, children will quickly learn and remain engaged. The large number of animals will keep kids busy and they will come back to their favorite animals over and over again.

The Good:

The app is simple to navigate and the illustrations are nice. There are 40 different animals, which is great for a free app. Parents don't need to pay to purchase additional animals or download a "full" version. Small children will enjoy hearing the animal sounds and watching each graphic's animation. Each page has a similar appearance, so kids will know exactly what to do on each screen. The background music also adds to the overall experience.

The Bad:

This is more of a "quiet" app in that the graphics, music and animation are nice, but don't make a big splash. Other than touching the animals to hear their authentic sounds, there isn't a whole lot to keep a small child's attention on the page. They will quickly move on to the next animal, so it's good there is a lot to choose from.

Additional:

This is an easy, educational app for small children that parents can add to their list. Kids will enjoy hearing the animal sounds and watching the animated graphics. With 40 different animal pages, it will give them plenty to explore.

Baby Flash Cards 450+ flashcards

Recommended Age Group: Toddler-Preschool

Grades:

- Educational—A-

- Fun—B+

- Overall—A-

Price: Free (No paid version)

Developer: eFlashApps

Compatible: iPhone

Review

What it is:

With more than 450 flashcards, "Baby Flash Cards: 450+ flashcards app for babies, kids in Preschool and Kindergarten!" covers a wide variety of categories using full-screen flash cards and even has an interactive game for kids to test their knowledge on what they've learned.

How it Works:

The main menu has 11 different categories of flash cards, including food, animals, letters, numbers, colors, transportation, clothing, furniture, parts of the body, objects and instruments. Select a category and a full screen photo of the first object in that category comes up (they are listed alphabetically). A voiceover says the name of the item and it appears in text across the top of the screen. Tap the screen to advance to the next flash card.

Some of the flash cards in certain categories include sound. For example, kids can hear the sound an animal makes, or the sound of an ambulance. The voiceover can be turned off in this app, and there is an option to have the flashcards rotate in random order.

There is also a "Question" mode that brings up four flash cards on the screen at once. The voiceover asks the child to click on the correct answer. When they do, the voiceover gives positive feedback, but if it's wrong, asks the child to try again.

What it Teaches/Develops:

This app teaches toddlers the words for more than 450 objects they encounter in their daily lives. They will learn by sight as well as by sound, and the repetition will improve their memory of these objects. They can also begin to recognize the words for them.

The Good:

This app covers a very large number of words in this free version in a wide variety of categories. The addition of sounds with some of the flash cards is a nice feature. The voiceover is clear and easy to understand. Kids can also go at their own pace and tap or swipe the screen when they are ready.

The Bad:

Unfortunately, many of the photos used in this app are not high resolution. They come out pixilated on the larger iPad screen. This app is also supported by ads that run across the bottom of the screen.

Additional:

This is an easy-to-use app for small children with a wide variety of words. There is an ad free version available for $1.99.

Musical Flash Cards - Animals

Recommended Age Group: Toddler-Preschool

Grades:

- Educational—B

- Fun—B

- Overall—B

Price: Free (Full version $0.99)

Developer: Kids Place

Compatible: iPhone

Review

What it is:

Even before small children start saying many words, they often make animal sounds, and "Musical Flash Cards—Animals images sounds and words for kids" will help them along. This app has a variety of favorite animal photos and their sounds for young kids to explore.

How it Works:

The app opens to a full screen of animal "flash cards," which are full color photos of animals in squares. There is a cat, dolphin, lion, parrot, chick, puppy, squirrel, elephant, cow, sheep, horse and duck. Touch one of the flash cards and it makes the animal sound, such as quacking for a duck. The word appears at the bottom of the screen. Touch the word and a voiceover says it. Instrumental music plays in the background, enhancing the experience. Kids can scroll down with their finger to see additional animal flash cards.

What it Teaches/Develops:

This app will teach very young children to recognize animals and their sounds. After spending some time with this app, they'll be able to correctly repeat the sounds after hearing them and identify the correct sound for each animal. Older kids will be able to recognize the word for each animal and correctly spell it.

The Good:

The flashcards use bright, colorful photos, the background music is pleasing and the animal sounds are easy to hear and authentic. The navigation is very simple and intuitive so that even babies as young as nine months old will be able to touch and play. The flash cards feature common animals that are associated with early learning for this age group.

The Bad:

The free version of the app only comes with the 12 animals listed above. The full version offers more than 65 animal flash cards, but they're only available as an in-app purchase ($0.99).

Additional:

If you're looking for an easy, entertaining app for your toddler, this is one they'll enjoy and can play entirely on their own. The photos of the animals are cute, and the animal sounds are fun to hear. If the full version is downloaded, then this is an app that will keep young children happy, busy and engaged.

Musical Flash Cards - Music Instruments

Recommended Age Group: Toddler-Preschool

Grades:

- Educational—B+

- Fun—B

- Overall—B+

Price: Free (Full version $0.99)

Developer: Kids Place

Compatible: iPhone

Review

What it is:

Kids love to explore the sounds of instruments, which makes "Musical Flash Cards—Music Instruments, images sounds and words for children" a fun app for young children. Simply by touching the photo of an instrument, they discover what kind of sound it makes.

How it Works:

The app opens to a full screen of musical instrument "flash cards," which are full color photos of different instruments in squares. There is an accordion, bagpipes, bass drum, bass guitar, bassoon, bell, bongo, conga drum, castanets, cello, clarinet and cornet. Touch one of the flash cards and it plays that instrument's sound. The word appears at the bottom of the screen. Touch the word and a voiceover says it. Kids can scroll down with their finger to see additional instrument flash cards.

What it Teaches/Develops:

This app teaches kids about different types of musical instruments and the sounds that go with them. They'll learn to recognize and identify an instrument by sight as well as by listening to it. Older kids will be able to recognize the word for each instrument and correctly spell it.

The Good:

The flashcards use bright, colorful photos and the sounds of the instruments are easy to hear and incredibly authentic. The navigation is very simple and intuitive so that even very young children will be able to touch and play. Many of the instrument names and sounds will be new for kids, so they will be able to learn and explore a wide variety of different musical instruments with this app.

The Bad:

The free version of the app only comes with only the 12 instruments listed above. The full version offers more than 45 musical instrument flash cards, but they're only available as an in-app purchase ($0.99).

Additional:

If you want to give your child an early introduction into musical instruments, this a great app. Young kids will really enjoy hearing the different sounds and being able to discover the instruments on their own. With the full version, they'll have an entire orchestra to explore right at their fingertips!

My First Words—Flashcards by Alligator Apps

Recommended Age Group: Toddler-Preschool

Grades:

- Educational—A+

- Fun— A+

- Overall— A+

Price: Free (Full version is My First 1,000 words-$1.99)

Developer: Innovative Mobile Apps

Compatible: iPhone

Review

What it is:

Teaching babies and toddlers beginning words is such an important development milestone, and "My First Words—Flashcards by Alligator Apps" does an amazing job at it. This app uses bright, colorful "flash cards" with voiceovers to help young children learn more than 200 common words.

How it Works:

There are a number of ways to use this app, all of which are accessed through the settings menu. In the "learn" mode, there are eight different ways kids can play, including words then flash cards, words then images, images then words, words only, flash cards only, and images only. There is also a "game" setting that includes recognizing and finding pictures, listening to find words and pictures and reading words to find pictures.

The main menu shows different categories of flash cards. These include actions, animals, baby things, feelings, food and toys. If you're in the "flash card only" learn mode, simply touch one of the categories and a full screen flash card appears. It will have a bright, colorful photo of an item and the corresponding word will appear in large, black type below it. A voiceover will also say the word. Touch or swipe the screen and another flash card in that same category appears.

Everything in this app is fully customizable. Parents can adjust the font size (enlarge it for babies), change the font color and whether or not the words appear in upper or lower case. They can also choose to let the kids change flash cards manually or let the app run it (in which case parents can also adjust how fast to go in between flash cards).

Additional customizable options include deleting any flash cards a parent might not want to teach their child, and creating their own flash cards by uploading photos. To take this even further, parents (or grandparents, siblings, etc.) can record their own voices saying the word that goes with the flash card.

What it Teaches/Develops:

This app will teach your baby or toddler the words for hundreds of different everyday items. They will be able to recognize the items from a photo and pick them out of a group; learn to say words and eventually recognize the words and read them. It is an interactive, dynamic way for kids to master these basic skills.

The Good:

This is a comprehensive, professionally made app that has a lot to offer parents and small children. There are a variety of words and the full screen flash cards are bright, colorful and attractive photos. The voiceover is clear and pleasant, and simple touch navigation is easy for any age to use. There is such a full range of customizable options, it gives parents multiple teaching tools all in one app.

The Bad:

This app will require that parents spend some time familiarizing themselves with all the settings. There are so many options, it's not one that very small children can set up on their own. Parents will want to make sure they find the right combination of font, size, color, speed and play mode to help children be successful so they enjoy the learning experience.

Although there are six categories of words included in this free app, there are seven additional categories that require extra purchase to unlock ($0.99).

Additional:

This is the kind of educational app that makes the iPad such a great learning tool. It's perfect for even the smallest children and teaches on multiple levels. With its fully customizable options, this is an app that every parent or grandparent with little ones should add to their list of best children's apps!

My First Words Baby Picture Dictionary

Recommended Age Group: Toddler-Preschool

Grades:

- Educational—A-

- Fun—B+

- Overall—A-

Price: Free (In-app purchase $0.99)

Developer: Teknowledge Software

Compatible: iPhone

Review

What it is:

To help teach babies and toddlers the words for common objects, "My First Word Baby Picture Dictionary" uses large photographs, a clear voiceover and simple navigation that will keep small children interested and engaged.

How it Works:

The main menu shows categories of objects using both words and pictures, including "Animals," "Baby Things," and "Food." Touch a category to bring up a full screen slide showing the picture of an object against a bright white background. A voiceover says the name of the object and the word is printed in black text below it.

There are small arrows at the bottom of the screen. Touch the arrow beside the word and the voiceover repeats the name of the object. Touch the arrow pointing to the right to advance to the next slide. Kids can also do this by tapping anywhere on the screen. To go back to the previous word, tap on the arrow pointing left.

If your child has a favorite object, touch the star in the upper right corner of the screen and it gets saved to the "Favorites" menu. All of the favorites can be played back from the favorites category off the main menu. There is also a "slide show" option from the settings menu that will automatically advance through all the pictures in a category without requiring the child to touch the screen.

What it Teaches/Develops:

This app helps the youngest children learn the words for more than 50 common objects found in everyday life. They can learn through repetition and the names are reinforced using both sight and sound.

The Good:

The pictures featured in the slide show are nice and large and the voiceover is very pleasing. Many of the pictures in the "Animals" category have accompanying animal sounds that play when children tap the animal on screen. There are a nice variety of pictures and words that not only appeal to small children, but that they encounter in their daily lives.

The Bad:

There is no background music or animation with this app. It is simply watching a slide show of objects and learning their names.

Additional:

There is a full version of this app for $0.99 that includes more than 250 words for categories such as clothing, colors, and shapes. If your child enjoys the pace and photos of this app, then the expansion pack would definitely be worth the small price.

Preschool Games—Farm Animals (Photo Touch)

Recommended Age Group: Toddler-Preschool

Grades:

- Educational—B+

- Fun—B+

- Overall—B+

Price: Free (No paid version)

Developer: GrasshopperApps.com

Compatible: iPhone

Review

What it is:

"Preschool Games—Farm Animals" is an educational app for very young children that uses real photographs to help them identify farm animals by sight, touch and sound. It's a simple app that even babies as early as 9 months of age can enjoy.

How it Works:

The main menu is simple, with just a "play" button to start. A full-screen, white background comes up with real pictures of farm animals (anywhere between 1 and 10 depending on the setting). A voiceover instructs to "touch the sheep" for example. When the correct animal is touched, a red circle pops up around it and the voiceover gives an encouraging remark, such as "perfect!" If the wrong answer is touched, then a sound effect signals to try again. After successfully completing a page, a new page comes up with a different set of animals and the same instructions as before.

As the child progresses through the animals, more choices of photographs are given each time (there are 18 possible animal photos). Many elements of this app are customizable. Parents can choose to include a display hint, which shows the word of the animal at the top of the screen. This is good for preschool aged children who might be learning to read.

There are also settings that allow parents to choose the minimum and maximum number of photos to display on the screen (between 1 and 10 for both). There is an option to delete any of the photographs as well as upload new ones, such as a family pet. Finally, there is an option to record additional sounds. These could include success and error sounds as well as animal sounds.

What it Teaches/Develops:

This app teaches very young children to identify pictures of common farm animals through repetition and begin to recognize the words for them as well. It teaches using visual and verbal cues and provides positive feedback when successful.

The Good:

The app uses real photographs that are professional quality and many of the farm animals are babies, so they really appeal to young kids. It is incredibly easy to navigate and the instructions are simple so that even babies can successfully play this activity. The customizable settings are good so that parents can adjust the levels according to age, and the recordable options for sounds and uploading unique photos is a great feature that makes this app unique.

The Bad:

While this app is helping kids to identify animals, it doesn't incorporate animal sounds into the activity. There isn't any background music either. It would be nice for kids to hear the sound the animal makes when they touch the photo of that animal.

Additional:

As long as parents adjust the setting levels accordingly to their child's skill, then this app will be a good fit for small children. The photos are fun and bright, the navigation is simple, and kids will enjoy playing this touch activity.

Shape Puzzle HD Free - Word Learning Game For Kids

Recommended Age Group: Toddler-Preschool

Grades:

- Educational--B+

- Fun—A-

- Overall—B+

Price: Free (Full version available $0.99)

Developer: Newness World

Compatible: Not with iPhone

Review

What it is:

Puzzles are a great way for kids to learn spatial reasoning, and "Shape Puzzle HD Free" is a great puzzle app to help with this concept. Toddlers put together the pieces of 15 different animal puzzles simply by dragging them into place.

How it Works:

Choose the forest scene from the main menu. A full screen graphic of the forest and animals come up. Touch an animal, such as the giraffe, and a new screen comes up with that animal cutout and surrounded by puzzle pieces to fill it in.

Select a puzzle piece and drag it to the correct location on the puzzle cutout. Once the animal puzzle is finished, a voiceover states the name of the animal and an animal graphic pops up with the animal name. Select the arrow to go back, and the forest has that animal filled in.

Each scene has 15 to 20 puzzles and each puzzle has 5 to 10 pieces. A wheel at the top of the screen provides an option to adjust the difficulty level of the game that includes easy, normal or hard.

What it Teaches/Develops:

This app focuses on a number of skills. It promotes spatial reasoning and teaches children the names of animals. It also encourages word recognition each time the name of the animal pops up on the screen.

The Good:

This is an easy-to-use, fun, puzzle app for toddlers. The jungle scene is filled with bright, cute animals to keep a young child's attention. The word reinforcement after completing each puzzle is a good addition.

The Bad:

Although it's easy to navigate into the app, there aren't any directions that help a child return to the main menu after an animal puzzle is completed.

Additional:

This is app is a great puzzle activity for any child under age 5. There is a full version available for $0.99 that includes at least nine scenes, and most kids will likely ask for more.

Physical Development

Puzzle apps for hand-eye coordination and spatial reasoning.

My first puzzles: Dinosaurs

Recommended Age Group: Toddler-Preschool

Grades:

- Educational--B

- Fun—B+

- Overall—B

Price: Free (Full version $1.99)

Developer: Alexandre Minard

Compatible: iPhone

Review

What it is:

For dinosaurs enthusiasts, "My first puzzles: Dinosaurs" is a fun app for preschoolers that delivers colorful dinosaurs with a variety of fun sound effects.

How it Works:

From the main menu select a level of play, either one, two or three stars. One star is the easiest level and a screen comes up with the outline of a dinosaur. Inside the dinosaur shape there are outlined areas that show shapes of each puzzle piece. The pieces are scattered around the dinosaur.

Select a puzzle piece and drag it into the right position inside the puzzle. If the piece does not fit, it moves away. During the game there are friendly sound effects to enhance the prehistoric theme of the game.

For the two and three star levels there is the additional challenge of assembling puzzles in order. Specifically, each puzzle piece shows a letter of the alphabet. The pieces only fit together in the order of the letters. When the puzzle is complete, a voiceover says the letters of the alphabet in order.

In this version of the app there are three puzzles for each level.

What it Teaches/Develops:

This app helps preschoolers with hand-eye coordination, spatial reasoning as well as learning the correct order of the letters of the alphabet and letter recognition.

The Good:

This app has bright, colorful graphics and fun sound effects that enhance the experience. The dinosaur theme is great for this age, and the varying skill levels is a good feature to ensure kids are playing at their correct skill level. The added challenge of putting the puzzle pieces together in alphabetical order is a great tie-in for reinforcing letter recognition and placement.

The Bad:

There is nothing bad about this app.

Additional:

"My first puzzles: Dinosaurs" is a fun way for preschoolers to develop their spatial reasoning skills and learn the alphabet. There is a full version of this app available with 36 additional puzzles for $1.99.

Whimsey: Lite

Recommended Age Group: Toddler-Preschool

Grades:

- Educational--B

- Fun—B

- Overall—B

Price: Free (Full version $0.99)

Developer: David Ross Software

Compatible: iPhone

Review

What it is:

For a completely different type of puzzle app, kids can try "Whimsey: Lite." Each puzzle is like putting together a "surprise," which is a photo of a different animal. Kids don't know what the puzzle is until all of the pieces are correctly moved into place.

How it Works:

The app begins with a full screen image of a puzzle outline and brightly colored puzzle pieces surrounding it. Select a puzzle piece and drag it into the correct position inside the puzzle. Outlines indicate where the pieces belong. If a piece doesn't fit, it goes back to the side of the screen.

When the puzzle is complete, it reveals a full-screen, compelling photo of an animal with the corresponding animal sound. This stays on screen for just a couple of seconds, until the shape of a new puzzle appears.

There are twelve animal puzzles inside this app. To get back to the home page tap the screen four times.

What it Teaches/Develops:

This app will help preschoolers with spatial reasoning as well as hand-eye coordination. It's fun for them to guess what type of animal each puzzle turns into.

The Good:

The app uses big, bold colors and highly captivating animal photographs. The shapes are easy to identify and simple for young children to manipulate into the correct spaces. Kids will also love being surprised each time the photo of the animal is revealed after completing the puzzle.

The Bad:

There are no menu options or additional features with this app, and there are only 12 puzzles to complete in this free version.

Additional:

"Whimsey: Lite" is a simple app that uses bold colored shapes and real animal photos to engage kids. There is a full version of the app available with sixty animal puzzles for $0.99.

Preschool-Kindergarten: 3 to 6 years old

Language & Literacy

Helps kids to read, spell, write, speak, listen and understand basic concepts.

Abby Train—Colors & Farm Animals

Recommended Age Group: Preschool-Kindergarten

Grades:

- Educational—B+

- Fun—B+

- Overall—B+

Price: Free (Full version $1.99)

Developer: CFC s.r.o.

Compatible: Not with iPhone

Review

What it is:

For preschoolers learning to recognize the names of their colors and animals, "Abby Train—Colors & Farm Animals" is a cute app that lets them be in charge of getting all the right answers on board the train as it chugs by!

How it Works:

The app opens by touching start in the middle of the screen. The next page is a menu with animal characters, and kids can choose which one they'd like to be. Touch it and the next screen is a colorful island setting with tropical music playing in the background. Kids can choose the "Farm" or "Colors 1" activity.

In the colors activity a large fish tank appears on screen with a number of sea animals in different colors. As the train chugs by at the bottom of the screen, a voiceover says a color, such as "red." The word also appears at the top of the screen. Touch the red colored fish in the tank and drag it to the train car at the bottom of the screen. The voiceover will give an encouraging comment and the point total will appear on the screen as well. With the next pass of the train, two colors will appear, followed by three colors.

The farm activity is similar, except that it is a farm setting and children have to place the correct farm animals into the train.

What it Teaches/Develops:

Preschoolers often have these types of lessons where they learn their colors, name of animals, etc. This app reinforces those lessons and even goes a step further by introducing the words for each at the top of the screen. It also encourages listening and following directions to make sure they get the correct answers onto the train.

The Good:

The graphics are very nice in this app, the sound effects of the train are fun and the voiceovers are clearly heard. The idea for the game is original, and kids will enjoy filling the train cars. It's also good that kids have to practice listening for more than one type of color or animal, and if they do forget, they can touch the word at the top of the screen and the voiceover will repeat it.

The Bad:

The animals don't always make it into the train cars when they're dragged across the screen, and it can take several tries. Also, when it lists more than one item, it doesn't matter what order they are put into the train. The app automatically puts it into the correct order that is listed on top of the screen. Part of listening and following directions is doing them in the correct order, a skill that is often emphasized at this age.

The free version only includes two activities: farm animals and colors. There is a full version available for $1.99 that comes with seven additional activities, including a second colors set, polar regions, yard, savanna, desert, sea and jungle.

Additional:

This is a unique app that is easy to navigate. Kids will enjoy the cute graphics and the concept of filling the cars on the train.

ABC first words

Recommended Age Group: Preschool-Kindergarten

Grades:

- Educational—B+

- Fun—B+

- Overall—B+

Price: Free (Full version $0.99)

Developer: Kids Place

Compatible: iPhone

Review

What it is:

Kids enjoy apps with music and a lot of animation, and "ABC first words—learn to spell musical instruments: Letters, Sounds & Writing fun game for children HD" incorporates both of these. Children can learn the sounds of the instruments and how to spell them using interactive letter building blocks.

How it Works:

The main menu gives two options: "classic" and "timed," which provides a little more challenge. Touch classic and a full screen background comes up of a famous world landscape. Over that is an ornate picture frame with a photo of a musical instrument in the middle, the first of which is a photo of "gongs." Building blocks with the letters that spell out "gongs" appear at the top of the screen. Then the blocks fall to the bottom of the screen. Kids use their finger to drag the blocks into the correct order back on top of the screen.

As each letter is touched, a voiceover says the letter. The blocks also make banging noises when they run into each other, and a sound effect indicates when the block is in the correct position. If it's not, then it falls back down to the bottom of the screen with the other blocks. Also, when the photo of the gongs is tapped, a gong noise plays.

When the word is complete, music plays and another screen comes up with the next musical instrument and its letters. For the "timed" activity, a small clock counts down the time it takes to correctly spell the word. If it's not done within one minute, the clock resets and the child gets another chance.

What it Teaches/Develops:

This app teaches kids how to spell different musical instruments and what they sound like. Since the letters are all provided, kids can also use their phonetic skills to try and sound out the words to spell them correctly.

The Good:

The app incorporates some very bright graphics and uses rather sophisticated animation with the falling blocks. There are a lot of sound effects, and the timed activity offers kids an added level of challenge that many will enjoy.

The Bad:

The animation on this app is very difficult to navigate. Kids are supposed to drag the letter blocks to the correct position at the top of the screen in order to spell the word. However, the blocks don't "drag" very well and unless they are placed in exactly the right position, they drop back down to the bottom of the screen. This is especially problematic during the timed activity. And in a few cases, the blocks got "stuck" together at the top of the screen.

Only three instruments come with the free version, yet there are 45 with the full version of the app.

Additional:

As long as kids don't get frustrated with the animation, then this app does have something different that they won't have seen before. It does have value from an educational perspective, and with the full range of instruments kids would enjoy the challenge it presents.

ABC Funnimals Lite

Recommended Age Group: Preschool-Kindergarten

Grades:

- Educational—A-

- Fun—A-

- Overall—A-

Price: Free (Full version $1.99)

Developer: Synthego

Compatible: iPhone

Review

What it is:

Learning the alphabet should be fun, and "ABC Funnimals Lite" does exactly that. Its kid-friendly graphics, humorous animation and great sound effects will engage small children and entertain them while teaching them the letters of the alphabet.

How it Works:

The main menu shows every letter of the alphabet. Touch any one of them to start and a full screen colorful background comes up. For example, touch "A" and a graphic of a cute ant comes up. A voiceover (which is a child's voice) says the letter, and then says "A is for Ant." The words also appear on the screen. Touch the graphic of the ant to see it try to lift an apple then fall down.

Touch the arrow at the bottom of the screen to advance to the letter B and see a new colorful graphic. The voiceover says the letter "B" followed by "B is for Bee." Touch the graphic of the flying bee and watch him get dizzy and float to the ground.

Arrows at the bottom of the screen advance forward and backward through the letters, and the return arrow at the top of the screen goes back to the main menu that lists all of the letters of the alphabet.

What it Teaches/Develops:

This app is a great way to teach toddlers their ABCs as well as introduce them to words that start with those letters, such as "ant" and "bee." It also introduces them to beginning phonics as they hear the initial sounds of those same words.

The Good:

This is a very easy app for kids to navigate. It's also incredibly appealing to small children. The child's voice as the voiceover is easy to understand but very endearing. The graphics are very well done, the sound effects are engaging and the animation is excellent. Each character does something humorous and unexpected will delight small children and keep them interested in finding out what the next one is going to do.

The Bad:

The only downside to this app is that this free version only has the letters A through F. For $1.99 parents can download the full version that has the entire alphabet. This app is so well done that both parents and kids will want the full version.

Additional:

In a market full of educational apps, this one really stands out. It's focused on teaching letter recognition to toddlers and does so using everything that appeals to the age group to keep them engaged: colorful graphics, fun sound effects and humorous content.

ABC Tracer—Letters, Numbers, Words, Phonics--FREE

Recommended Age Group: Preschool-Kindergarten

Grades:

- Educational—A-

- Fun—A-

- Overall—A-

Price: Free (Full version $1.99)

Developer: App-Zoo

Compatible: Not with iPhone

Review

What it is:

Learning to write letters using the correct strokes is so important for kids to learn as they enter Kindergarten. "ABC Tracer—Letters, Numbers, Words, Phonics—FREE" not only helps kids practice this concept, but it goes a step further to reinforce recognition of letters and words.

How it Works:

The colorful main menu has eight different activity options. These include tracing uppercase letters, tracing lowercase letters, tracing numbers, tracing words, learning the ABC song, "popping" alphabet balloons, matching beginning letters to pictures and a painting activity.

For each of the tracing activities a colorful full screen graphic comes up of a friendly lion holding two sheets of white writing paper. The app demonstrates the correct way to write the letter on the left sheet of paper then the child has a chance to repeat it on the right sheet. Dots outline the letter and kids trace simply by using their finger. Fun music plays while they trace, and if they use an incorrect stroke, the app gives gentle clues. Once the letter is complete, the page advances to the next letter.

For the ABC song activity, kids can choose to have the app sing the song and they can watch the letters of the alphabet dance, or they can explore the letters on their own. In the popping balloons activity, kids much pop the alphabet letters in the correct order by touching them. When they do, the balloon reveals a graphic that starts with that letter.

For the matching activity, four pictures come up on the screen and a letter of the alphabet is at the bottom. Kids much touch the picture that starts with that letter. Finally, in the painting activity, kids can use their finger to color a picture. The word for that picture is at the bottom of the screen, which can be traced and colored as well.

There is also a settings menu that allows parents to choose a preference of the stroke order for tracing, as well as options for showing dotted versus solid lines, saying the letter when it shows, clapping for success and auto advancing when a letter or word is complete.

What it Teaches/Develops:

This app really focuses on teaching kids the correct way to write numbers and letters, both in upper and lowercase. It also reinforces number, letter and word recognition using common associations such as "a for apple" and "b for ball."

The Good:

The interactive component of this app is very good. Kids will love tracing with their finger and the clapping and cheering when they're successful is a nice touch. There are a good variety of activities that really complement each other in reinforcing the educational aspects of this app. The sound effects are fun, the graphics are appealing to kids and the activities are age appropriate.

The Bad:

Tracing with fingers can be tricky, and there isn't a lot of room for error. If kids don't get the letter just right, the app can stall, leaving kids wondering if they traced it correctly or not. And other than the clapping and cheering for tracing a letter correctly, there is no other award system to motivate kids to be successful.

In this free version of the app it only gives the first four letters of the alphabet, A through D, and the numbers 1 through 4. There are also only four coloring pictures with the paint activity and a few letters for the popping activity.

Additional:

This is a nice app to help kids learn the proper strokes for writing numbers, words and letters. It's easy for little hands to do on their own and provides a wide variety of fun activities, which all reinforce letters, writing and phonics.

Amazing Match (LITE): Kids Favorite Word Learning Game

Recommended Age Group: Preschool-Kindergarten

Grades:

- Educational--B+

- Fun—B+

- Overall—B+

Price: Free (Full version $0.99)

Developer: Joy Preschool Game

Compatible: iPhone

Review

What it is:

Match games are a great way for kids to improve their memory skills, and "Amazing Match (LITE)" is an easy-to-use app perfect for younger kids. Preschoolers will be challenged to match the pictures hidden underneath the tiles and get as many matches as they can.

How it Works:

There are four matching games to choose from: hamburger (bakery), watermelon (fruits), ambulance (vehicles), rocking horse (toys), and four levels of difficulty--easy normal, hard, and super.

The game starts with a set number of tiles that are blank on the front. Tap a tile to turn it over and reveal a picture. Tap a second tile to see if it's the same picture or a different one. Continue tapping tiles until all of the matches are found.

When the tiles match, the app enlarges the picture on the tile and shows the word of the picture in text below it. A voiceover also says the word.

If the two tiles chosen don't match, they both flip back to their original positions and kids select two more tiles. Correct matches get positive points and incorrect matches get negative points. When all of the matches are correctly done, there is a final score.

What it Teaches/Develops:

This app helps preschoolers develop their concentration and memory skills. It also helps them learn to recognize the words for objects and how to spell them.

The Good:

This app is very easy to use. It starts up without any menu choices, and has fun, bright graphics. The game is simple and provides a great way for kids to be challenged and test their memory skills.

The Bad:

There is nothing bad about this app.

Additional:

"Amazing Match (LITE)" will keep preschoolers engaged with its simple game play. There is also a full version available for $0.99 that has 15 different scenes with colorful graphics.

Animal Preschool Word Puzzles HD

Recommended Age Group: Preschool-Kindergarten

Grades:

- Educational—B+

- Fun—B+

- Overall—B+

Price: $1.99 (Free version available)

Developer: CFC s.r.o.

Compatible: Not with iPhone

Review

What it is:

Kids love to solve puzzles and "Animal Preschool Word Puzzles HD" gives a new twist to a classic game. By rearranging letters in the correct order, kids are able to put the puzzle pieces together to form a picture of an animal.

How it Works:

After choosing the start button for the puzzle activity, kids can choose from 11 different settings: backyard, farm, meadow, forest, castle, polar regions, desert, jungle, sea, savanna I, and savanna II. Each setting has its own unique set of animals. Choose one of the settings, and a full screen graphic comes up. Each animal appears as a silhouette. Touch one of them to solve the puzzle.

The puzzle screen has vertical segments, each with a piece of the animal picture and one of the letters that spells the word for that animal. Touch one of the segments and a voiceover says that letter. Slide each segment into place to correctly spell the word and complete the picture of the animal. When it's done correctly, a voiceover says the word and gives an encouraging statement. Touch the back button on the screen to choose another animal from that setting.

The main menu also has a button called "My animals," and all the animals that are completed show up on that screen. There is also a settings menu that allows parents to choose all uppercase, lowercase or capitalized letters, as well as the mode for solving the puzzle. "Insert" mode simply places the puzzle piece in the spot indicated and the rest of the pieces move one space to the right. "Swap" mode replaces the piece moved with another piece.

What it Teaches/Develops:

This app teaches letter and word recognition. It is also an introduction to phonological awareness as they try to sound out the animal words to put the letters in the correct order. As they're doing this, they are also reinforcing their knowledge of animals and their sounds.

The Good:

The settings are bright and fun and the animal characters are cute and appealing to young kids. The concept of solving a puzzle is good, especially since kids have to both put the pieces in the correct order to complete the picture and spell the word at the same time. With 11 different settings to choose from, there are a wide variety of animals that will keep children's interest. And it's nice that there is a type of reward system with the "My animals" page so that kids can go back and see how all of the different animals they've collected.

The Bad:

This app is aimed at the preschool and kindergarten age levels, but many of the words are too difficult for these age groups. Some of the animals, such as "dog" and "cat" are age appropriate, but very few will be able to spell "orangutan" on their own. They can get some visual clues through the picture, but some kids may get frustrated and not stick with the activity for long.

The app would really benefit from having a "help" button that could either show kids the correct spelling or give them some type of clue. It would also be nice if in addition to the voiceover saying the letter when it's tapped the sound of the letter were stated as well. This might go one step further in helping kids sound out the longer words to spell them correctly.

Additional:

This app has a lot to offer young kids, especially those who enjoy challenges such as puzzles. It has a good educational approach and kids will certainly learn from it. As long as the difficulty level doesn't frustrate them at times, it should be an app that they will want to play often.

Articulation Station

Recommended Age Group: Preschool-Kindergarten

Grades:

- Educational—A

- Fun—B+

- Overall—A-

Price: Free (No full version but can purchase additional sounds in-app.)

Developer: Little Bee Speech

Compatible: Not with iPhone

Review

What it is:

For parents and teachers looking for a tool to help children with speech articulation, "Articulation Station" is the perfect app. Using bright, colorful graphics, an easy interface and a variety of teaching activities, kids will enjoy practicing their speech sounds.

How it Works:

The app offers a full set of instructions including a video tutorial, which is helpful for getting started. The app offers 22 speech sounds, including some blended sounds. The main menu lists all of the sounds. Simply touch the targeted sound to start.

If your child needs to practice the sound, there is a sound card for each one. Touch it and a voiceover says the sound. There is also a tip sheet for ways to practice the sound. At the bottom of each sound card is a list of activities: words, sentences and stories. Words can be practiced using either flashcards or by playing a matching game. With the flashcards, a photo and word come up that use the target sound. Touch the photo and a voiceover says the word. Swipe the screen for the next flash card. For the matching game, touch two cards to find the matching set of pictures. Each picture uses the target sound.

In the sentences activity, flash cards come up that have sentences in which multiple words use the target sound. Touch the card and the voiceover reads the entire sentence. For the stories activity there are two levels. Level 1 uses simple sentences and pictures, all with the target sound. Touch each sentence and the voiceover reads it. Level 2 stories are for kids who can read. They are longer and don't have any pictures. There is a quiz kids can take at the end to answer questions about the stories.

For all of the activities parents and teachers can choose whether the target sound is in the initial, medial or final position of the word. The app will keep track of up to six users, and each can be scored and have their progress tracked in the program. There is also a recording option so that answers can be played back and monitored.

What it Teaches/Develops:

This app teaches children speech articulation in up to 22 sounds using a variety of activities. Each one focuses on using the target sound in either words, sentences or stories. It also lets the child practice the sound in either the beginning, middle or end of words.

The Good:

This app has a wide variety of activities that all focus on helping kids to articulate an individual sound. Parents and teachers can modify the app to best fit the needs of the child and can track the child's progress along the way. The graphics are bright, the activities are fun and kids will enjoy working with an interactive program that they can easily navigate.

The Bad:

This free version of the app only includes one sound, the letter "P." All of the other sounds are available as in-app purchases. Although it's understandable that not every child would need to practice all 22 sounds, most teachers and speech professionals would want all of them as part of their teaching tools.

Additional:

Parents who want to give their child extra help in speech articulation can purchase just the sounds they need. Educators who work with many children at once would be better off purchasing the entire program. Either way, this app has a lot to offer, and kids will benefit the most in the end.

Dora's Skywriting ABC's

Recommended Age Group: Preschool-Kindergarten

Grades:

- Educational—B+

- Fun—B+

- Overall—B+

Price: $3.99 (No free version)

Developer: Nickelodeon

Compatible: iPhone

Review

What it is:

In this app, Dora and Boots help kids with recognizing letters, the sounds they make, and how to write the letters.

How it Works:

Dora provides direction throughout the app with the help of Boots. Tico uses his Nutty Plane to write letters and draw pictures of objects.

The first step in the app is tracing. Your child traces the Nutty Plane over nuts to create a letter. When the tracing is done, a letter is revealed. Dora says the name of the letter and the sound it makes.

Next, your child learns the name of an object that starts with this letter. Your child tilts the iPad to place nuts in the holes that outline this object. When all the holes are filled in, the object is slowly revealed.

Your child has three levels to choose from: uppercase, lowercase and upper and lowercase letters.

What it Teaches/Develops:

This app teaches children the alphabet and how to write letters.

The Good:

This app uses the popular character, Dora, to involve young kids to learn. The games are easy-to-use and adding in the physical play of tilting the iPad makes it more involving.

The Bad:

There is nothing bad about this app, although some kids may find the animation repetitive.

Additional:

Children will be attracted to this app because of the popularity of Dora. The app is simple to use as young kids can easily trace a plane and tilt the iPad to learn letters of the alphabet.

First Letters and Phonics

Recommended Age Group: Preschool-Kindergarten

Grades:

- Educational--B

- Fun—B

- Overall—B

Price: $1.99 (Free version available)

Developer: Learning Touch

Compatible: iPhone

Review

What it is:

One of the first ABC activities preschoolers learn is the alphabet song, and "First

Letters and Phonics" is a good compliment to that. To help kids learn the alphabet, this app uses bright pictures for each letter, a voiceover saying the letters and several versions of the ABC song that kids will enjoy.

How it Works:

When First Letters and Phonics is opened, there are two options: "Play the Game" and "Play the Song." In "Play the Game" kids are greeted with instructions that read "To play, drag each tile to its match. Match all the letters to hear a song!"

For example, a tile comes up with the letter "a." Drag it to another tile with the same letter "a." When the match for the "a" is made an apple appears and a voice says, "A, is for apple." The game continues for each letter of the alphabet.

When the entire alphabet is complete, Debi Derryberry, a popular children's musician sings the alphabet song (A,B,C,D...). When a letter of the alphabet is sung, it is enlarged and centered on the screen and kids can sing along.

The "Play the Song" activity takes kids directly to the alphabet song. There is also an options menu to select features including one to three tile pairs shown, upper/lowercase letters, the speed of the song, and even a phonics version where the alphabet song is sung phonetically.

What it Teaches/Develops:

This app teaches preschoolers to recognize the letters of the alphabet as well as their phonetic sounds. It accomplishes this with the repetition of single letters in the game, the letters to form a word, and in the alphabet song.

The Good:

The app is simple to use and focuses solely on the letters and sounds of the alphabet. The letters are easy to read and the graphics are bold and bright. Hearing the ABC song played at the end is a good reward for kids who match all of the letters correctly. The customizable options are good so that parents can make adjustments according to their child's level.

The Bad:

Although the app is very simple and easy for preschoolers to navigate, it's very repetitive.

Additional:

"First Letters and Phonics" is a good app to help small children learn the alphabet. There is also a Lite version available that parents can download for free and try it out with their child first.

FirstWords: Sampler

Recommended Age Group: Preschool-Kindergarten

Grades:

- Educational--B+

- Fun—B+

- Overall—B+

Price: Free (Full version $4.99)

Developer: Learning Touch

Compatible: iPhone

Review

What it is:

Help preschoolers learn how to spell their first words with "FirstWords: Sampler." In this app, kids drag letters to form the word of the object shown. They can play all on their own or the app will provide hints to help them along.

How it Works:

Each full screen page shows a cute illustration. Underneath the drawing are blank boxes, one for each letter of the word. There are also tiles for letter on the screen. Kids must drag each letter tile into the correct blank box to spell the word. Whenever they touch a letter, a voiceover says the name of the letter.

When the word is correctly spelled, the voiceover reinforces the spelling by stating each letter in order and the word that it spells. At the same time, the object illustrated spins around, gets bigger, and makes a noise associated with the object.

There are many options in this app including selecting the length of the words, letter order, and letter hints, which shows where each letter is supposed to be placed. As an additional benefit there are five language options: English, French, German, Japanese, and Spanish.

What it Teaches/Develops:

This app helps preschoolers with a number of language and literacy skills, including letter recognition and sounds, word recognition and reading. It also helps improve their hand-eye coordination as they drag letters across the screen.

The Good:

This app has very colorful graphics and entertaining animation after kids complete the words. The voiceover is a good reinforcement for hearing the letters and sounds, and the navigation of the app makes it easy for kids to play on their own, especially when the hints are turned on.

The Bad:

The app does not let you get back to the home page after you start playing.

Additional:

FirstWords: Sampler is a fun app for children to learn letters, spelling, words and even sounds. There is a full version of the app available with 147 words for $4.99.

iKid: Lessons Lite

Recommended Age Group: Preschool-Kindergarten

Grades:

- Educational—B+
- Fun—B+
- Overall—B+

Price: Free (Full version $1.99)

Developer: Fresh Factory

Compatible: iPhone

Review

What it is:

For a unique app that helps kids observe a scene and test their knowledge on what's happening, "iKid: Lessons Lite" uses colorful characters and animated graphics to create an engaging activity. Touch each part of the scene to hear and see what it is, then listen to the questions and touch the correct parts to answer.

How it Works:

This free version of the app includes the "theater" activity, which focuses on emotions. Kids are on stage acting out "The Three Little Pigs" play. Other kids are in the audience watching. Touch anywhere on the screen to hear a voiceover describe what it is and see the word in text at the top of the screen. Then touch the question mark to hear the voiceover ask a question about the scene. Touch the part of the scene that answers the question.

Once all of the questions are answered, kids can touch the "rotate" icon in the top right corner of the screen and the theater scene changes, giving kids new parts of the scene to explore and answer questions.

The graphics are animated and background music plays during the activity. There are also multiple language options to choose from, including English, Russian, German, French and Italian.

What it Teaches/Develops:

This app teaches kids how to observe what they see, listen to what is described and then be able to answer questions about it. It's a good activity to practice their comprehension skills, especially as a precursor to reading comprehension.

The Good:

This app uses appealing characters and nice graphics. The concept it teaches is very good, and the feature of having the scenes rotate is good because it makes kids have to pay attention to new details and recognize the changes in the scene. The questions involve being able to identify objects, action and emotions.

The Bad:

The voiceover on this app has a dialect that's made some of the words difficult to understand, especially for small children who may not be familiar with different accents. Also, each version of the scene only has about six questions, and these repeat over and over again.

Additional:

This app is a good way for kids to practice their listening and comprehension skills. If they like the game, parents will want to purchase additional individual scenes for $0.99 or purchase the entire set of four scenes for $1.99.

iWriteWords (Handwriting Game)

Recommended Age Group: Preschool-Kindergarten

Grades:

- Educational—A-
- Fun—A-
- Overall—A-

Price: $2.99 (Free version available)

Developer: gdiplus

Compatible: iPhone

Review

What it is:

Learning how to write letters and numbers using the correct strokes is important for preschoolers, and "iWriteWords (Handwriting Game)" is the perfect app to help them practice. With cute graphics and visual guides, kids can practice writing their letters and numbers.

How it Works:

The main menu shows a solid green screen with small dots in the bottom right corner that are the activity options. Kids can choose to write numbers, individual letters in both upper and lowercase or write letters that spell words in both upper and lowercase.

For the individual letter activities, a bright colored screen comes up with the outline of a letter such as "A." There is a tiny crab in the corner of the letter and several colored dots with numbers on them that pop up around the outline of the letter. Kids use their finger to drag the crab and collect the numbers, writing the letter as they do. When the letter is complete, they get to slide it into the hole and advance to the next letter. Parents can choose either upper or lowercase letters.

For the word activity, kids practice writing letters that spell a word, such as "cat." Once they have written all of the letters and completed the word, a cute child-like drawing of a cat pops up on screen and kids can slide all of the letters into the hole. There are more than 70 words available.

There is also a song activity where kids tap the screen to play each note of the ABC song.

To access the settings menu, go to the main iPad settings. From there parents can adjust the handwriting style, the degree of difficulty in writing, which require more accuracy and turning off or on uppercase words.

What it Teaches/Develops:

This app helps kids practice writing letters and numbers using the correct order of strokes. They can write both upper and lowercase and there is a setting to adjust the width of the drawing path. This would be helpful for younger kids who might need a larger space to write whereas older preschoolers can fine-tune their writing.

The Good:

This is a fun concept with graphics that really appeal to preschoolers. A majority of kids won't have any trouble successfully helping the crab collect his dots in order to write the letter or number. Having options for both upper and lowercase is good, and being able to adjust the degree of difficulty is a good way to challenge kids.

The Bad:

For an app aimed at preschoolers the navigation is not very simple. There are no verbal instructions and a lot of small children won't intuitively know how to work the app. Parents will need to show them how to drag the crab to collect numbers and how to slide the letters into the hole when they're done.

Additional:

The drawing mechanism on this app is good—wherever your child's finger goes, the lines go. And if kids go the wrong way or don't make a complete stroke, the app gently helps them. It's a fun way for kids to learn how to write.

Kids Learning-Photo Touch Concepts

Recommended Age Group: Preschool-Kindergarten

Grades:

- Educational--B
- Fun—B
- Overall—B

Price: $0.99 (No free version)

Developer: GrasshopperApps.com

Compatible: iPhone

Review

What it is:

In addition to learning about colors, letters and numbers, preschoolers need to understand concepts such as above/below, big/small and same/different. "Kids Learning-Photo Touch Concepts" is an easy-to-use app that helps children learn these concepts using bright photos and easy navigation.

How it Works:

Select "Play" to start the app. A screen appears with several photos. A voiceover asks a question and instructs to touch the photo that is the correct answer. The question also appears in text across the top of the screen.

For example, two identical photos of a dog appear and the voiceover asks to "touch the dog on the right." If your child selects the wrong dog, there is a noise signaling the choice is incorrect. If your child selects the correct dog, the voiceover provides positive feedback and another screen appears with another question.

One question is asked per screen. After a correct answer, the app automatically advances to a new screen with a new set of pictures. This continues until your child exits the game.

There is a settings menu accessible from the main menu that allows parents to select sound, hints, voiceover reinforcements and up to twelve concepts for kids to practice.

What it Teaches/Develops:

This app teaches preschoolers a range of concepts using sight, touch and sound along with bright photos of everyday items. The concepts covered include above/below, right/left, right/middle/left, big/small, short/tall, top/middle/bottom, directions and which one is different.

The Good:

This is an easy-to-use app that encourages kids to listen and understand these important concepts. As kids play, the activity automatically increases in complexity, giving kids greater challenges so they don't become bored. The customizable options are also a good way for parents to adjust the app according their child's ability level.

The Bad:

There is nothing bad about this app.

Additional:

"Kids Learning-Photo Touch Concepts" is an app that focuses on a specific set of concepts that kids need to understand. It is easy for children to use, provides them with positive feedback and is a fun educational tool.

Little Speller-Three Letter Words LITE

Recommended Age Group: Preschool-Kindergarten

Grades:

- Educational--A-

- Fun—B

- Overall—B+

Price: Free (No paid version)

Developer: GrasshopperApps.com

Compatible: iPhone

Review

What it is:

"Little Speller-Three Letter Words" helps young students learn beginning spelling concepts using simple, three-letter words and easy touch-screen navigation in a fun, friendly learning environment.

How it Works:

Kids can immediately start using the app simply by pressing the "play" button. A large picture comes up on the screen, for example a bus, and then three letter tiles are displayed on top of the image. A voiceover says what the image is and the word to be spelled. The tiles are randomly placed and may even lie on top of each other. Beneath the image are spaces where the tiles go, indicated by indentations and outlines of the letters. This helps kids who are learning to spell visually match the letters and place them in the correct spaces.

As each letter is dragged into place the voiceover tells the child what the letter is, for example the letter B, U and then S. Once the word is complete the voiceover says, "you did it, you spelled the word bus." Then the letters are repeated in sequence as the letters "jump" in place.

What it Teaches/Develops:

This app helps teach preschoolers spelling as well as letter and word recognition. As the foundation of both reading and writing, spelling provides exposure to new concepts through symbols (words).

The Good:

This app focuses on common, simple three-letter, one syllable words that children encounter daily. The images help reinforce what they are learning, and the navigation is simple and easy for young children to figure out on their own.

The Bad:

It'd be nice if this app did systematic letter recognition rather than just identify letters in the context of the words being spelled. However, that might distract from the focus of helping children learn words.

The settings include some advanced options, but there aren't clear instructions for these. These functions include longer words, upper and lower case letters, setting the puzzles to alphabetical or random, custom lists, editing game sounds and even customizing the letters themselves. Despite the lack of instructions, parents should spend some time customizing the app so it's appropriate to their child's skill level.

Additional:

For parents with preschoolers who are ready to learn how to spell simple, everyday words, this app is a good starting point and one to add to the list of easy educational apps.

Mini-Adventures—Let's Go and Learn the Alphabet

Recommended Age Group: Preschool-Kindergarten

Grades:

- Educational--B+

- Fun—A-

- Overall—B+

Price: Free (No paid version)

Developer: Innovative Mobile Apps

Compatible: iPhone

Review

What it is:

Kids love interactive multi-media, and "Mini-Adventures—Let's Go and Learn the Alphabet" delivers a very good product. This is an educational app that teaches younger children letters and word recognition using a compelling combination of high-quality photos and videos. It takes full advantage of the iPad's glossy, high resolution LCD screen, giving your child an engaging, vibrant experience.

How it Works:

At start-up, kids can choose to "browse" through the full list of photos, which are in alphabetical order, or start on a random photo. A full-screen picture appears, such as a "race car," with the letters of the word spelled out underneath in boxes. An accompanying voiceover says the word and is highlighted in red. A small video player appears in the upper left corner of the screen. Touch it and a larger video window pops up. The video, smartly obtained from YouTube, features a one to three-minute clip of the object in motion. When the video is finished, the original photo and word reappear on the screen.

When your child taps the photo, a new picture of a similar object appears, along with a new video. Each word has several photos and videos (totaling more than 500) giving kids multiple experiences. To get to a different word, simply swipe the page and a new photo appears. Another option is to touch one of the letters in the word. This will bring up a photo of a word that starts with that letter. For example, touch the "a" in "race car," and a photo and video of an airplane might come up.

What it Teaches/Develops:

This app helps children with letter recognition and beginning letters in words. There are quite a few images that many children probably aren't familiar with, such as an "omnibus" or "maglev," and the videos help provide context so kids will understand what the word means.

The Good:

The photos are full color, superior quality and artistic. The videos, all from YouTube, are also high quality and professional (not grainy "home videos"), with full sound, including music. The content is appropriate for young children, and the videos are interesting, unique and many are action-packed.

The Bad:

All of the words, photos and videos in this app are transportation related. It's an interesting approach and lends itself to some cool videos. However, videos of monster trucks crushing cars, sports cars at auto shows and boys performing tricks on razor scooters may make the app more appealing to boys.

Some of the words and photos aren't as dynamic as others. A photo of a "van" doesn't seem exciting enough to prompt kids to want to watch the video. And the video of a "donkey" walking in a circle may not stimulate them to explore the word further and watch additional "donkey" videos.

Additional:

With multiple videos for more than 120 words, any child will find something fun to watch. While the teaching component is geared more for younger children, kids of any age (as well as parents) will enjoy the videos. In fact, some of them are so entertaining, your kids will likely want to watch them over and over again.

Mini-Adventures—Animals

Recommended Age Group: Preschool-Kindergarten

Grades:

- Educational—A-

- Fun— A-

- Overall— A-

Price: $0.99 (No free version.)

Developer: Innovative Mobile Apps

Compatible: iPhone

Review

What it is:

Kids and animals go hand-in-hand, making "Mini-Adventures—Animals" a fun app for all ages. Using high-quality photos and videos of a wide variety of animals, this app teaches children letters and word recognition. The bright, colorful photos and educational videos will engage your child and provide a lot of enjoyment.

How it Works:

At start-up, kids can choose to "browse" through the full list of photos, which are in alphabetical order, or start on a random photo. A full-screen picture appears, such as a "dog," with the letters of the word spelled out underneath in boxes. An accompanying voiceover says the word and the letters are highlighted in red. A small video player appears in the upper left corner of the screen. Touch it and a larger video window pops up. The video, smartly obtained from YouTube, features a one to three-minute clip of the animal. When the video is finished, the original photo and word reappear on the screen.

When your child taps the photo, another photo of that same animal appears, along with a new video. Each word has several photos and videos (totaling more than 1,000) giving kids multiple experiences. To get to a different word, simply swipe the page and a new photo appears. Another option is to touch one of the letters in the word. This will bring up a photo of a word that starts with that letter. For example, touch the "g" in "dog," and a photo and video of a goat might come up.

What it Teaches/Develops:

This app helps children with letter and word recognition and beginning letters in words. It features favorite animals like dogs and cats, along with some lesser-known species, such as the "ibex" and "quoll." Most letters of the alphabet feature multiple animals (the letter "s" has 28 different animals), which provides valuable repetition for teaching letters.

The Good:

The photos are full color, superior quality and artistic. The videos, all from YouTube, are also high quality and professional. In fact, many of the videos are from TV productions, made by National Geographic, major zoos and other nature/animal programs. A majority of videos are very educational and teach facts about animals that kids will find fascinating.

The Bad:

While certain animals are going to attract kids, like the tiger, horse or puppy, other animals are not going to be as popular, such as the fly, goldfish or crow. Kids will be tempted to skip these videos and go straight for the "larger than life" animals, missing out on some really well produced videos that have a lot to offer.

Unfortunately, some of the animal videos are a little boring. Several clips of a woodpecker pecking at a tree or perched on a rail aren't going to keep your child's attention. And there is one animal, the "urial," that even though it has several nice photos, it doesn't have a single video to watch.

Additional:

With multiple videos for more than 120 animals, all kids will find a number of videos to watch featuring their favorite animal. This is an app where kids are going to get much more out of it than just learning letters and words. There are so many interesting animal facts on the videos, it's an app that the whole family can enjoy.

Montessori Crosswords—Learn Spelling with Phonics

Recommended Age Group: Preschool-Kindergarten

Grades:

- Educational—A-

- Fun—B

- Overall—B+

Price: $2.99 (No free version)

Developer: L'Escapadou

Compatible: iPhone

Review

What it is:

When it comes to spelling and phonics, "Montessori Crosswords—Learn Spelling with Phonics" knows how to do it right. This app uses a combination of words, images and sounds to help kids improve their phonetic letter sounds and spelling.

How it Works:

The app menu has three levels to choose from: simple words, words with consonant blends and complex words. In simple words, an image appears, such as a "bag" with three blank spaces beside it. Letters of the alphabet are displayed along the bottom of the screen. There is also a "help" section in the upper right corner. Text directions are given to show kids what to do. If you touch the image, a voiceover says the word "bag." If you touch the first blank square, the voiceover gives the sound for the letter "b." Touch and drag the "b" from the alphabet along the bottom of the screen and put it in the correct square. Sounds indicate whether or not the letter is correct. If help is needed, touch the upper right square and the correct spelling of "bag" is displayed. Once the word is correctly filled in, an animated screen comes up. Floating stars, hearts or flowers fill the screen and kids can "move" them around.

For the "consonant blends" and "complex words" kids can choose between a single word and multiple words in crossword style (one word going across the screen and a second word going down the screen). The two words share a common letter in "crossword" style.

There is also the menu option to have the words all focus on a certain sound, such as a short "a" or long "i," and there is a setting called "movable alphabet" that lets kids explore letters and sounds on their own. The 3.5version of the app even includes an option with Christmas words.

There are even settings that allow you to change font, including uppercase, lowercase and cursive. You can also change the alphabet display from regular alphabet order to the QWERTY keyboard order and even vowels listed first followed by the rest of the alphabet.

What it Teaches/Develops:

This app is great at helping kids master their letter sounds. It also teaches younger children simple spelling, while allowing slightly older kids to work on more difficult words and exploring letters and creating words on their own.

The Good:

With so many different settings and levels, this app is a great teaching tool for kids that fall within a wide range of abilities, as is often the case at this age. The help feature is nice to have so they can enjoy it just as much as kids who can spell. The graphics are bright, the sound effects are pleasing and the interactive component is simple but fun. The animation at the end of each round is a unique and creative way to reward kids when they're successful.

The Bad:

For kids who don't yet know how to spell, they may have a tendency to use the "help" box right away. While they will still learn letter sounds, they won't benefit from the challenge of trying to correctly spell the words on their own. Also, some kids may have a harder time hunting for the correct letters at the bottom of the screen and may ask for assistance.

The app doesn't change "pages" very quickly and at times the animation seems to get "stuck" on the page, overlapping with the next set of words.

Additional:

With so many levels and settings, this app is a wonderful phonics tool for kids across multiple ages. It uses common words and easily identifiable images. It gives kids a dynamic, interactive experience and includes a fun reward system.

Phone for Kids—All in one activity center for children HD

Recommended Age Group: Preschool-Kindergarten

Grades:

- Educational—A-

- Fun—B+

- Overall—B+

Price: Free (Full version in-app $1.99)

Developer: Kids Games Club

Compatible: iPhone

Review

What it is:

Kids love to play on their parent's phone, and "Phone for Kids—All in one activity center for children" lets them feel like a grown-up. With a number of interactive learning activities, this app helps teach children some basic concepts while having fun at the same time.

How it Works:

The main menu has six initial picture buttons, each representing a different activity. There are seasons, ABCs, directions, phone, painting and text chat. There are four additional buttons along the bottom of the menu screen. These are the "sing and learn" buttons. Each one plays a different note (do, re, mi, fa) when tapped.

The activity starts with a full screen winter scene. Lively holiday music plays in the background, and a voiceover says "winter," while the word appears at the bottom of the screen. Touch the screen and a snowball shows up that "splats" on the screen with a sound effect. Kids can "throw" as many snowballs as they like. After about 20 seconds the scene changes to "spring." Touch the screen and this time "flowers" pop up in the field. At the summer beach scene butterflies float across the screen when touched, and for autumn leaves fall with the wind blowing sound effects. Tap the home button on the bottom right corner of the screen to go back to the main menu.

The ABC game allows kids to "type" on a QWERTY keyboard. For each letter they touch a voiceover says the letter and it appears in the middle of the screen. The directions activity brings up a large compass. Touch the screen and a voiceover says a direction, such as north, and the word appears on the screen in the appropriate location (at the top for north). Touch the compass and it "spins" around. The phone activity brings up a phone dial pad. Kids can "type" in a number with realistic key tones then tap the phone key and it "rings." Touch the animated phone in the bottom left corner and it brings up a different dial pad with new sounds, including music for the pound and star keys.

The paint activity allows kids to draw with their finger on a full screen white canvas. Ten different color options are at the bottom of the screen. Touch any one to draw in that color. The text activity brings up another QWERTY keyboard. This time kids can type in a message and press "send." Their message appears above the keyboard on the screen, which simulates a real text conversation on a cell phone.

What it Teaches/Develops:

This app provides a number of simple educational activities for young children. It helps them learn seasons and cardinal directions both visually and with words; letter recognition; creativity with drawing; familiarity with numbers on a phone dial pad and learning the numbers 0-9.

The Good:

This app offers a number of quick, simple activities that young children can easily do by themselves. The backgrounds are colorful, the sound effects realistic and the music is fun and lively. Several of the apps really do simulate a "phone," which kids will enjoy, and the variety will keep them busy.

The Bad:

The free version of this app only gives the six different activities described above, but there are 18 additional activities available as in-app purchases, including balloon numbers, animal quiz, treasure map and color car race.

Additional:

Variety is the key to keeping young children entertained, and this app offers a number of simple, quick activities that kids can do on their own. Many of them are educational and age appropriate, and with the full version, kids will really enjoy playing this one over and over again.

Preschool: 15 in 1 Kids Pack

Recommended Age Group: Preschool-Kindergarten

Grades:

- Educational—A-

- Fun—B+

- Overall—A-

Price: $1.99 (No free version)

Developer: Deepak Demiwal

Compatible: Another version for iPhone for $0.99

Review

What it is:

For the preschooler who likes a variety of simple, fun activities, "Preschool: 15 in 1 Kids Pack" is an app that will keep them busy and make them happy. The activities include drawing, writing letters and numbers, identifying animals and playing games like matching and hangman, and all are done using colorful graphics and animation.

How it Works:

The main menu is bright, colorful and easy to follow. Each activity is easily found and there is even an "instructions" button that parents can read through to find out exactly how to do each one. The "sketch book" activity brings up a full screen blank "paper" with options along the bottom that lets kids choose their color, type of brush and a "picture" if they want to color one in.

The "Animal Kingdom" activity brings up a screen with a number of simple animal graphics. Touch one, and a voiceover says the name of the animal followed by the sound it makes. There are more than 50 animals to choose from. "My First Step" includes both alphabet and number "flash cards" that use simple graphics and a voiceover to help kids identify them. In "Learn to Write" kids can trace letters and numbers with their finger, even choosing what color to use.

"My First Word" has a little different approach to learning words. A picture comes up on the screen with the accompanying word below it, but its letters are "missing" (they are simply in black text). The letters are scrambled at the bottom of the screen and kids drag the letters to their correct spaces to spell the word.

"Calendar" uses simple songs to teach both the days of the week and the months of the year. The "Math" activity teaches addition, subtraction, multiplication and division through a multiple choice approach. Finally, there are three "Games" kids can play. These include matching, which has easy, medium and hard levels; hangman, which shows the picture of the word as a clue; and the exam, which quizzes kids on their colors and shapes.

What it Teaches/Develops:

This app teaches young children a variety of basic concepts including number and letter recognition; animal sounds; word identification; colors and shapes; math; and helps improve memory as well as creativity with drawing.

The Good:

There are a lot of educational activities in this app that small children will enjoy, especially the matching and hangman games. The colors are bright and the graphics simple but appealing to small children. The instructions for parents are a nice added feature as well.

The Bad:

The drawing animation on this app isn't very precise. In the "Learn to Write" activity it can take several attempts at tracing the letters and numbers in order to complete it correctly. And in the "Sketch Book" activity the drawing tools aren't very fluid. This app also doesn't include any music in the background or extra sound effects that enhance the experience.

The Math activity in this app is way beyond the preschool level, especially compared to the simplicity of the other activities. Not many preschoolers will be able to solve the equations. It has no voiceover and the "hand written pencil" graphics are even difficult to read.

Additional:

This is a good app that offers something for any preschooler. It's very educational, simple to navigate and has bright, fun graphics. Parents and kids will be pleased with this all-inclusive activity pack app.

Sight Words by Photo Touch

Recommended Age Group: Preschool-Kindergarten

Grades:

- Educational--A

- Fun—B+

- Overall—A-

Price: Free (No paid version)

Developer: GrasshopperApps.com

Compatible: iPhone

Review

What it is:

Any parent familiar with sight word flashcards will love "Sight Words by Photo Touch." This is an easy-to-use app that helps kids learn to read the most common sight words based on seeing the written word and hearing a vocal prompt.

How it Works:

Select "Play" to launch the app. Three boxes appear on screen with a different sight word in each box. A voiceover says one of the words. Touch the word in the box that matches the word said, and the voiceover provides positive reinforcement such as "great job" or "perfect."

There is one question per screen. The app automatically increases the level of difficulty be adding additional boxes with words, and the app continues until your child exists.

There are customizable options with this app. Parents can select the level of words, sound, minimum number of items to display, voice-over reinforcements, and more.

What it Teaches/Develops:

This app helps teach kids to recognize and read common sight words, which is a necessary assessment they need to pass in school. They learn the words by both sight and sound.

The Good:

This app is very easy for kids to navigate and a great educational tool. There are a wide variety of levels to select from, all the way from preschool to third grade sight word lists. There is even a customizable option for parents to record their own voices reading the words, or even add their own words, making the app more personal and fun for kids.

The Bad:

There is nothing bad about this app.

Additional:

"Sight Words by Photo Touch" is an app that provides kids an excellent way to learn how to read individual words. It is easy for children to use and provides them with positive feedback.

Sight Words List - Learn to Read Flash Cards & Games

Recommended Age Group: Preschool-Kindergarten

Grades:

- Educational--A-

- Fun—B

- Overall—B+

Price: Free (No paid version)

Developer: Innovative Mobile Apps

Compatible: iPhone

Review

What it is:

"Sight Words List—Learn to Read Flash Cards & Games" uses interactive flashcards to teach children common sight words in an easy to navigate environment.

How it Works:

After the app is launched a full screen black board comes up with a number of options. The top row of options relates to the grade level of the child using the app including "Preschool," "Kindergarten," "First Grade," "Second Grade," and "Third

Grade." There is also an option to select "Nouns." The second row of options includes features for "Favorite" and "Shuffle."

To start the game, select a grade level. A screen comes up with the first flashcard. A word appears on the card and a voiceover says the word. To advance to the next flashcard, touch the screen. To save the flashcard as a favorite, tap the star in the top right corner of the screen. These can be accessed from the "Favorite" button off the main menu.

By selecting "Shuffle," the app shuffles flashcards from the different grade levels. To get help for the app, select the "i" on the top left of the home page. To get to the list of options select the wheel icon. These include sound, speed, looping and much more. Parents can also customize the flashcards to keep kids challenged with new words, and anyone can record their own voice saying the words.

What it Teaches/Develops:

This app helps teach kids to recognize and read common sight words, which is a necessary assessment they need to pass in school. They learn the words by both sight and sound.

The Good:

This app is very easy to navigate and includes a wide variety of common sight words. The option to add additional words is a great way to increase kids' range of words and improve their reading ability.

The Bad:

Some children may become bored with simple flashcards on a screen.

Additional:

There are more than 315 sight words in this app, and with the ability to add more, parents have a free app to add their list of educational tools.

Word BINGO

Recommended Age Group: Preschool-Kindergarten

Grades:

- Educational--A

- Fun—A

- Overall—A

Price: $0.99 (No free version)

Developer: ABCya.com

Compatible: iPhone

Review

What it is:

"Word BINGO" is an app with four games in one that help children learn to recognize sight words. Play Bingo, practice spelling, stop blocks from building up and fling bugs—all fun games that kids will enjoy playing.

How it Works:

For the Bingo game a screen comes up with a bingo card filled with sight words. A voiceover says one of the words. Tap the word to mark it. Once a child has four correct words in a row vertically, horizontally or diagonally they get a Bingo.

There is a score provided at the end of each game that is based on the time needed to complete the game and the number of incorrect answers. In addition, when kids have a high score, the reward is a Bingo Bug. These Bingo Bugs are saved on another screen where kids can make them spin and move around.

For the Spelling Practice game tap and drag letters in the corresponding boxes to spell a word given by the voiceover. Boxes outline each letter to make it easier, and only the correct letter fits into a box. When the word is complete, the voiceover repeats the word.

For the Fling It game, kids must find as many BINGO Bugs as possible in a one hundred second time period and fling them to hit an object called a warp zone. To find a BINGO Bug, tap on the word given by the voiceover.

For the Word Up game kids need to stop falling word blocks from stacking up to the top of the screen. A voiceover says a word and kids must tap the block with that word to make it disappear. Tap on the wrong block and it stays stacked on the screen.

The app also allows for up to five players and one guest. There is a scoreboard that tracks the top three scores for each level of game play.

What it Teaches/Develops:

This app teaches a number of important concepts. It helps kids learn and recognize sight words, spelling and reading. It also helps develop listening and comprehension skills as well as following directions.

The Good:

This is a fun app for children with challenging and interesting game options. It is helpful that the voiceover gives clear direction at the start of each game, and the reward system is a good feature. The graphics are bright and colorful and games can be adjusted according to age level and ability.

The Bad:

The Fling It and Word Up games are only accessible after the Word Bingo game is completed.

Additional:

This is a very good app that provides kids with a variety of ways to learn their sight words. It goes a step beyond just recognition and encourages them to be able to spell the words as well. Kids will have fun playing the different activities and being rewarded in the process.

Interactive Books

Promotes a positive attitude toward books and encourages kids to read.

Cowboys and Aliens: The Kids

Recommended Age Group: Preschool-Kindergarten

Grades:

- Educational—A-

- Fun—A-

- Overall—A-

Price: $1.99 (No free version)

Developer: ISBX

Compatible: iPhone

Review

What it is:

"Cowboys and Aliens: The Kids" is a true interactive children's book app with a fun, rhyming story, professionally created full-color illustrations, and extra activities that will entertain kids across many age groups.

How it Works:

To begin the story from the main menu, simply touch the green "forward" arrow at the bottom of the screen. The first page of the story comes up, which is a full screen colorful illustration with some animation. The story text appears at the bottom of the screen. Touch the "play" arrow to hear a narrator read the text and see the words highlighted as they are read. Tap any word twice to hear and see it spelled as well. Kids can also touch different parts of the page to hear additional sounds and see hidden animation. Touch the green "forward" arrow again to turn the page.

After the story is finished, kids can explore additional activities on the main menu by touching the green button at the top of the page. From here they can paint coloring pages of each of the illustrations, record their own voice reading the story text, upload photos of themselves to replace the faces of the story characters and even share these pages with others.

The settings menu has options for turning on and off the background music, the young reader mode and savings the recordings and coloring pictures.

What it Teaches/Develops:

This app is a great bridge for kids between traditional print books and digital books. It encourages reading for older kids but also has the narration option for preschoolers who aren't yet reading. It promotes listening and comprehension skills and after the story is finished, the coloring pages serve as a tie-in activity to keep kids engaged in the story.

The Good:

This is truly an interactive book complete with hidden animation that kids will enjoy discovering. The illustrations are equal to any traditionally published picture book, and the story is fun and age appropriate. Having the extra activities is a great way to keep kids interested in the app even after the story is finished.

The Bad:

The story is rather short and doesn't take long to read. Once kids have listened to it a few times and found the hidden extras, they might not come back to it again. They are more likely to play with the paint and photo activities.

Additional:

This story app really raises the bar for interactive children's book apps with its animated illustrations. In an app market flooded with games, this is a great one for parents to download so that younger kids have a book they can read "on the go" all by themselves.

Forest Friends

Recommended Age Group: Preschool-Kindergarten

Grades:

- Educational—A-

- Fun—B+

- Overall—A-

Price: $4.99 (No free version)

Developer: DJ International

Compatible: Not with iPhone

Review

What it is:

"Forest Friends" is a multimedia experience for kids. The app includes a movie, two stories, coloring pages and music that all feature illustrated forest animals in a friendly setting.

How it Works:

All of the options are listed on the main menu that features the forest characters: movie, book, friends, piano and coloring. Touch "movie" and it launches a full-screen animated movie about "Moe the mole" who is looking for his squirrel friend, Sammy. There are voiceovers for each unique character, simple animation and subtitles at the bottom of the screen.

Under the "book" category there are two stories: "Where are you, Sammy!" and "Find the Acorns!" Each story features "Moe the mole" and his forest friends in a cute tale. The text is printed on each page and kids turn the page by swiping across the screen with their finger.

The "friends" activity brings up a forest setting with each of the characters partially hidden. Touch each one to bring it out of hiding and see a cute animation. Touch it again to find out who it is.

The "piano" activity brings up several large keys from a piano. Each one has a picture of one of the forest friends. Touch a key to hear it play. Kids can play their own songs with the forest friends.

The "coloring" activity includes several coloring pages featuring the forest friends. Kids can choose a paint color and brush to color in the picture.

What it Teaches/Develops:

This app promotes reading in preschoolers and encourages them to explore an interactive book in a variety of ways. It makes the experience of engaging with a book more dynamic and provides kids with multiple opportunities to connect with the characters and the story.

The Good:

This app features very nice illustrations and friendly forest animals. The variety of activities is good for keeping kids entertained. The animated illustrations are fun and the voiceovers and background sound effects enhance the overall experience.

The Bad:

The navigation in the app is a little confusing. The swiping mechanism to turn the pages during the story is not inherent. The movie is narrated but the stories are text only, so preschoolers who are not reading would have to have an adult read the story to them.

Additional:

This app provides preschoolers with a nice set of activities that all revolve around central characters and the story. It's a good concept and nice way to encourage kids to spend time reading.

Goldilocks and the Three Bears—Kidztory animated storybook

Recommended Age Group: Preschool-Kindergarten

Grades:

- Educational—A
- Fun—A-
- Overall—A

Price: $0.99

Developer: Stepworks

Compatible: iPhone

Review

What it is:

"Goldilocks and the Three Bears—Kidztory animated storybook" is a classic and a great way for kids to experience reading using the latest form of digital media. With wonderful illustrations, surprise animation and options to read with and without narration, there is a lot to explore in this story.

How it Works:

From the main menu select "read to me" or "read by myself." For kids who aren't yet reading on their own, the "read it to me" is the perfect option. Each page is fully illustrated with the words in black text across the screen. A cute child voiceover narrates the story. Parts of the illustration are animated, and kids can touch areas of the screen to find hidden sound effects. To turn the page, simply touch the forward arrow at the bottom of the screen.

The "read by myself" option work just like the "read to me" option, but the voiceover doesn't narrate the story.

What it Teaches/Develops:

This app promotes reading, listening and comprehending stories, as well as fosters a positive attitude toward books. It provides kids with a dynamic, interactive reading experience.

The Good:

This app has wonderful, kid-friendly illustrations, nice animation and fun sound effects. The child voiceover will appeal to small children and having options to have the story narrated or for kids to read it by themselves are great features

The Bad:

There are no negatives for this app.

Additional:

This is a true interactive book that even the smallest readers will enjoy. There is a whole collection of classic stories as interactive book apps available from this developer, which would be worth browsing.

Green Eggs and Ham

Recommended Age Group: Preschool-Kindergarten

Grades:

- Educational—A

- Fun—A

- Overall—A

Price: $3.99 (No free version)

Developer: Oceanhouse Media

Compatible: iPhone

Review

What it is:

Anyone who loves classic Dr. Seuss books will love this interactive book of "Green Eggs and Ham." The app looks exactly like the its book version but adds professional narration, sound effects and highlighted text, giving kids numerous ways to explore each page.

How it Works:

From the main menu select one of three options: "Read to me," "Read it myself," and "Auto play." During the "Read to me" option professional narrators read the text using different voices for each character in the story. The classic Dr. Seuss illustrations are on each page, and music plays in the background. Touch any individual word and it is highlighted. Touch any of the pictures on the page and the voiceover says what it is, and it shows up in text on the screen as well. To turn the page, swipe the screen from right to left as though turning an actual page in a book.

The "Read it myself" option eliminates the narrators, but all the other extras are still available. The "Auto play" option is similar to the "Read it myself" option but the pages automatically turn.

What it Teaches/Develops:

This app promotes reading, listening and comprehending stories, as well as fosters a positive attitude toward books. It provides kids with a dynamic, interactive reading experience.

The Good:

This app maintains all of the classic illustrations found in the original version of Green Eggs and Ham, but enhances them with fun sound effects and learning extras. The options to have the story narrated or for kids to read it by themselves are great features.

The Bad:

The only possible downside to this app is that text does not accompany the story. However, adding text would have compromised the wonderful graphics and animation.

Additional:

This is a true interactive book that even the smallest readers will enjoy. There is a whole collection of classic Dr. Seuss stories as interactive book apps available from this developer.

Nighty Night! HD

Recommended Age Group: Preschool-Kindergarten

Grades:

- Educational—A

- Fun—A

- Overall—A

Price: $1.99 (No free version)

Developer: Shape Minds and Moving Images GmbH

Compatible: Not with iPhone

Review

What it is:

"Nighty Night! HD" is an amazing interactive story that provides a truly unique experience for kids. With incredible 2D animated graphics, a professional narrator and a sweet tale, kids will love exploring this app as part of their bedtime routine.

How it Works:

Press "start" from the main menu and the app launches into an animated scene overlooking a town where lights are turning off in all the houses, except for a farmhouse. The narrator begins telling the story, which subtly includes instructing the child to turn off all the lights in the different parts of the farm. Touch any of the lights in the window to change screens and see a new animated screen of an animal in that part of farmhouse. Touch the animal to see and hear it do fun animations. Then touch the light switch to turn out the light and put the animal to bed. Continue for each animal, including a dog, pig, sheep, duck, cow, fish and chickens, until the end of the story.

There are options from the main menu to turn the narration on or off. With the narration off, kids can explore the farmhouse without listening to the story. There is also an "autoplay" option that plays the animation straight through. There is no story, but the narrator does say "nighty night" to each animal as the lights are turned off.

What it Teaches/Develops:

This app encourages children to listen to a story and be an active part of that story. The extensive animation allows kids to explore many aspects of the tale and experience it in their own way.

The Good:

This app has beautiful 2D graphics that go way above and beyond most interactive books. It plays more like a movie than a book, and provides a true interactive experience. The story is cute and age appropriate, the animals are funny and the narration by actor Alistair Findlay is phenomenal.

The Bad:

The only possible downside to this app is that text does not accompany the story. However, adding text would have compromised the wonderful graphics and animation.

Additional:

With its wonderful message, soft lullaby music and pleasing graphics, this bedtime story will be a favorite for small kids. The biggest challenge may be getting your child to stop playing and actually go to bed.

PopOut! The Tale of Peter Rabbit

Recommended Age Group: Preschool-Kindergarten

Grades:

- Educational—A
- Fun—A
- Overall—A

Price: $4.99 (Free version available)

Developer: Loud Crow Interactive Inc.

Compatible: iPhone

Review

What it is:

"PopOut! The Tale of Peter Rabbit" is an interactive book that takes the classic story of Peter Rabbit and provides a level of interaction unlike any other. Kids can "pull" and "slide" tabs to see pictures "pop" out and "rotate" to life.

How it Works:

The main menu has options for kids to read the story themselves or have it read to them. Touch "start" and the story's book cover opens to reveal the beautifully illustrated pictures from the original book. For kids who want the story read to them, a professional narrator reads while the words in the text are highlighted.

Kids can touch the illustrations to see animation. On many pages there are small "tabs" with visual instructions to pull or slide them, similar to what actual pop up books have. When kids move the tabs, certain illustrations slide or pop out. Swiping the corner of the screen will turn the page in the story.

What it Teaches/Develops:

This app promotes both listening and comprehension when hearing a story as well as reading and recognizing words. The pop outs help kids to experience the story as would in a real book, enhancing their experience and understanding of the story.

The Good:

This app has managed to successfully recreate the beauty and joy of the original Peter Rabbit story. Kids will forget they're not reading an actual book. It's one of the best representations of a traditional book available as an app.

The Bad:

There is nothing negative about this app.

Additional:

This developer has done an amazing job with this interactive book and has a number of other interactive book apps available, including many of the popular Sandra Boynton stories, which kids love.

Read Me Stories - children's books

Recommended Age Group: Preschool-Kindergarten

Grades:

- Educational--B+

- Fun—B+

- Overall—B+

Price: Free (interactive stories at $1.99 each)

Developer: 8Interactive Limited

Compatible: iPhone

Review

What it is:

Imagine giving kids an entire library of books to read. That's the concept behind "Read Me Stories--Children's books." This free app provides kids with a way to sample an interactive book from seven different series, and then the option to buy their favorites.

How it Works:

There are seven series of books and between 5 and 29 books in each series. The series are: Tuffy's First Adventure (5 books), Tuffy's Second Adventure (5 books), Tales of Adventure (23 books), Animals I (14 books), Animals 2 (13 books), Tales of Life (29 books) and Songs (5 books). The first book in each collection is free with this version of the app.

To preview a book in a series, scroll between the collections by swiping the screen. Next, tap an illustration from a series to preview it. Then tap the book cover to begin reading.

A voiceover narrates the book. In some series the words in the book are highlighted with the characters in the book coming to life. In other series the narrator simply reads the story.

To prevent your child from buying a series by accident, there is a verification system to ensure adult approval.

What it Teaches/Develops:

This app helps to make reading fun for kids. It reinforces word recognition and encourages them to spend time exploring a wide variety of books.

The Good:

This app provides a free book sample from each series. The stories are entertaining and the illustrations for each collection are big and colorful. With so many different types of stories, there will be something that interests every child.

The Bad:

It was disappointing that their entire library was not available yet.

Additional:

"Read Me Stories--Children's books" is an excellent way for your child to have fun reading interactive books anytime they want. Parents can find out which series their kids like and buy a series starting at $.99. The Tuffy Adventures are the newest series available from this developer.

The Monster at the End of This Book...Starring Grover!

Recommended Age Group: Preschool-Kindergarten

Grades:

- Educational—A

- Fun—A

- Overall—A

Price: $3.99 (No free version)

Developer: Sesame Street

Compatible: iPhone

Review

What it is:

"The Monster at the End of This Book...Starring Grover!" is a fully interactive, animated version of the classic Sesame Street story by the same title. Not only does it engage kids, but also parents can interact with their child while reading this lovable story.

How it Works:

The main menu provides guided instructions. After launching the app, an animated Grover leads kids through the story. He doesn't want them to turn the pages of the book because there is a monster waiting at the end. As Grover speaks, his words appear in text and each word he says is highlighted.

There are plenty of opportunities for kids to engage in the story. For example, Grove ties ropes around the pages to prevent kids from turn them, but if they tap on the knots, they come undone. Grover is good about giving verbal instructions on what to do next.

There is a parent tip button in the upper right corner of the screen that provides suggestions on ways for parents to engage in the story. For example, ask your child what he/she is afraid of? There is also an option in the settings menu, located as a button in the upper left corner of the screen that enables "young reader mode." This provides helpful visual clues to younger children.

What it Teaches/Develops:

This app promotes both listening and comprehension when hearing a story as well as reading and recognizing words. If parents use the hint button, they can engage their child in critical thinking. The entire app helps kids explore the story in a fully interactive environment in their own way.

The Good:

For kids who are familiar with Sesame street and enjoy the popular books with Grover, they will love this animated interactive book version. Grover has the same voice he uses on the TV show, and the story itself is fun for young kids. The app is structured in a way that makes it easy for parents to play with their kids, which is a nice way for them to experience an activity together.

The Bad:

There is nothing negative about this app.

Additional:

Sesame Street has a long history of providing quality entertainment for kids with an educational emphasis. This app upholds those high standards and is a great way for kids and parents to enjoy an interactive book together.

The Princess and the Pea

Recommended Age Group: Preschool-Kindergarten

Grades:

- Educational—A

- Fun—A

- Overall—A

Price: Free (In-app purchase $0.99)

Developer: TabTale LTD

Compatible: iPhone

Review

What it is:

Kids will love helping the handsome "prince" find the perfect princess in "The Princess and the Pea—An Interactive Children's Story Book HD." This app is an animated interactive book complete with full-color illustrations, animation and engaging narrator.

How it Works:

Kids can choose to have the story read to them or to read it themselves. There is even an autoplay option that plays the entire story without having to turn pages. For the narrated story, a voiceover reads the text that is also displayed at the top of the page. (There is an option to hide/unhide the text as well). As the narrator speaks, each line of text is highlighted.

Kids can also touch different parts of the illustration to see animated graphics and hear sounds. For example, touch the queen to see her place the pea under the princess's mattress. There are also other interactive activities throughout the story, such as helping the princess try on different dresses.

What it Teaches/Develops:

This app promotes both listening and comprehension when hearing a story as well as reading and recognizing words. The story engages children and the interaction with the animated graphics helps them understand what the story is about.

The Good:

This is a fun approach to a classic story. The illustrations are very bright and colorful, the narration is well done and the animation is fun. The extra activities make the interactive book even more dynamic and enjoyable for young children.

The Bad:

This is an app geared more toward girls, although many boys will enjoy the humorous animation within the story.

Additional:

For a free app this is a nicely done book. There is a full version for $0.99 that is ad-free. Although the ads are small at the bottom of the screen, if parents don't want children' accidentally clicking on them, they may want to consider the full version.

Toy Story Read-Along

Recommended Age Group: Preschool-Kindergarten

Grades:

- Educational—A

- Fun—A

- Overall—A

Price: Free (Paid version for Toy Story 2 and Toy Story 3 Read-Along.)

Developer: Disney Publishing Worldwide Applications

Compatible: Not with iPhone

Review

What it is:

Little fans of the movie "Toy Story" will love "Toy Story Read-Along." This app turns the movie into a full interactive story complete with text, music, coloring sheets and games. There are lots of activities to keep kids busy playing with Woody and Buzz Lightyear.

How it Works:

For the story, there are several modes to choose from, including a "read to me" with a narrator and a "young reader mode" that displays the text on the screen and highlights as its being read. There is also an option to have the pages turn automatically. Kids can also record their own voice reading the story.

For several of the page illustrations, there is an option to color them as a picture. Kids can paint their own colors or choose to paint the picture to match what is in the story.

For kids who are familiar with the songs in the movie, there are two sing-along songs. There are also two games that kids can play. One that features the toy army men in which kids try to navigate the parachutes down the ground and a maze to help Buzz and the toys escape from the toy barn.

What it Teaches/Develops:

This app promotes both listening and comprehension when hearing a story as well as reading and recognizing words. The addition of the coloring, music and game options give kids a variety of way to experience the story.

The Good:

This is a fun app for any child who is familiar with the Toy Story movies. The character voices and illustrations are all the same from the movie. The extra activities are a great way for kid to really engage and experience the app on multiple levels.

The Bad:

There is not as much animation on the story pages as with some other interactive books, but kids will still love hearing the story.

Additional:

This is a great free app for fans of Toy Story. There are a number of ways to interact with the characters and it's done in a rich, dynamic way that kids will love.

Math

Teaches kids to count, sort, recognize patterns, and how to add and subtract.

01 Kids Builder HD FREE: Joy Preschool

Recommended Age Group: Preschool-Kindergarten

Grades:

- Educational—B+

- Fun—A-

- Overall—B+

Price: Free (Full version $0.99)

Developer: Joy Preschool Game

Compatible: Not with iPhone

Review

What it is:

Preschoolers are natural engineers, and "01 Kids Builder HD Free: Joy Preschool" gives them the tools they need to "build" colorful structures. Bright, colorful landscapes, cute characters and extra surprises make this app a different delight for both boys and girls alike.

How it Works:

The main menu presents an inviting selection of "structures" to build, including a castle, Ferris wheel and merry-go-round. Select the castle, and a full-screen background comes up. It includes a castle in a green field with a merry-go-round and Ferris wheel set underneath a starry evening sky. A cute hippo is also there to help the child along. A voiceover gives instructions to "click on the shining frame to find out the right shape." Touch it, and the voiceover names the shape. Next a banner of shapes pops up and the child must touch the matching shape. If correct, then the hippo places it on the structure and another shape "shines." Once all of the structures have been "built," fireworks explode in the sky, kids cheer and the hippo waves his arms.

There are two extra features that can be accessed from the main menu. One is a present button that takes kids to a screen that shows the rewards they've won for completing a build. They can get exploding fireworks, balloons and dancing lollipops. The hippo button takes them to a screen filled with all of the shapes used in the buildings. Touch one, and the voiceover names it, then it explodes into a firework in the night sky.

What it Teaches/Develops:

This app will help preschoolers learn and recognize a number of shapes, including square, rectangle, triangle, oval, star, heart, parallelogram and trapezoid. They must also listen for the verbal instructions and be able to match the "shining" shape to the one in the banner.

The Good:

The graphics are really appealing to this age group and kids will enjoy "building" and completing a scene. Familiar background music plays with each landscape, including "Twinkle, Twinkle, Little Star." There is a lot of cute animation, such as flipping fireflies and a squirrel zipping down a slide on the playground. Additionally, when kids drag their finger across the screen, they can create ribbons of stars.

The Bad:

This app teaches a number of shapes, but a few have confusing labels. The circle is called "round" rather than "circle," there is one called "curve" rather than an arch and another that is called "zig zag."

Additional:

This is a cute app that really focuses on helping teach preschoolers their shapes. It's a fun idea with a number of hidden extras that kids will enjoy.

Abby—Basic Skills Preschool: Puzzles and Patterns HD

Recommended Age Group: Preschool-Kindergarten

Grades:

- Educational—B+

- Fun—B+

- Overall—B+

Price: Free (Full version $1.99)

Developer: 22Learn, LLC

Compatible: Not with iPhone

Review

What it is:

Preschoolers can get on board with "Abby—Basic Skills Preschool: Puzzles and Patterns HD." They can help "Abby" the monkey fill her train with toys by completing the activities and have fun in the process.

How it Works:

After touching "start" off the main menu, "Abby," who is a train conductor, appears on screen and explains how to play. There are two activities: puzzles and patterns. Abby drives a colorful train with four train cars across the screen and stops in the middle. Either a puzzle or pattern activity appears above the train. For the puzzle, kids have to drag puzzle pieces into the correct spots to complete a picture of a toy. Once it's done, the toy goes into a train car.

For the pattern activity, a series of toys appears on the screen. Kids have to choose which toy completes the pattern from a variety of toys and then drag it to the correct place. Once it's done, then that toy goes into another train car.

Once kids have completed four activities and all four train cars are full, then they get to choose a sticker to put on the sticker board. They also get to design the next train by choosing four different colorful train cars from a group.

What it Teaches/Develops:

This app teaches preschoolers some of the basic fundamental math skills they need to learn at this age. They learn spatial reasoning from the puzzle activity and patterning. The repetition helps reinforce the concepts to ensure they have a good understanding of them.

The Good:

This is a fun app with cute graphics and age appropriate activities. Kids will have fun filling up the train cars and getting their sticker rewards. Letting them design their own train is also a neat addition. There are verbal instructions for each activity so kids know exactly what to do. And for younger kids who might need a little help, there is a setting parents can turn on that displays a picture of the correct answer in the corner of the screen.

The Bad:

This version of the app only has two activities, but the full version of the app has 10 complete activities, which are available as in-app purchases.

Additional:

Although limited in the number of activities, this is a fun app that preschoolers will enjoy. It's easy to navigate, has good sound effects and animation. It's also educational and provides kids with a cute reward system.

Bugs and Buttons

Recommended Age Group: Preschool-Kindergarten

Grades:

- Educational—A

- Fun—A

- Overall—A

Price: $2.99 (No free version)

Developer: Little Bit Studio, LLC

Compatible: iPhone

Review

What it is:

"Bugs and Buttons" uses these items in a creative combination to provide fun, interactive games and activities that kids will love to explore. There is so much to do in this one app, it will keep preschoolers engaged for long periods of time and they'll want to come back for more.

How it Works:

The main menu has icons for 18 different games and activities, all featuring high quality, colorful backgrounds and graphics, animation and playful music. Some of the activities include flinging bees at a flower target, flying a butterfly through an obstacle course, playing tic tac toe with a dragonfly, sorting buttons on a conveyer belt, racing roaches, catching falling buttons, solving bug mazes, counting bugs and catching colorful lightning bugs in a jar.

Each time a level is completed, the child earns a bug stamp for their collection. There are more than 40 stamps available. Visual instructions are provided for the activities, and the longer kids play, the more challenging the games become. For example, when sorting buttons on the conveyer belt, the higher the level, the faster the belt moves.

What it Teaches/Develops:

This app teaches children a number of critical learning skills. In mathematics, they learn counting, classification and sorting, and recognizing patterns. They must also use their problem solving skills for activities such as the bug mazes and tic tac toe. The app is so interactive, it also helps children develop their fine motor skills.

The Good:

All of the games and activities in this app are creative, educational and extremely fun. The graphics are bright, colorful and dynamic. The music and sound effects enhance the experience, and the interactive components are diverse but all age appropriate. The bug stamp collection is a great reward system and the adaptive level of play is good so that kids remain challenged.

The Bad:

This app is void of any bugs (except for the ones that are supposed to be on the screen!)

Additional:

The idea of using only bugs and buttons is so simple, but this app goes above and beyond. To find an educational game that will truly entertain kids is worth so much, and this is one that parents, and kids, won't want to miss.

Monkey Math School Sunshine

Recommended Age Group: Preschool-Kindergarten

Grades:

- Educational—A

- Fun—A

- Overall—A

Price: $0.99 (No free version)

Developer: THUP Games

Compatible: iPhone

Review

What it is:

"Monkey Math School Sunshine" is an app that will make your preschooler smile. Brightly colored animation, lively island music and a cute monkey mascot help make this educational app one that young kids will enjoy while learning basic math concepts.

How it Works:

The app starts up quickly simply by touching "play." The first activity comes up on the screen and verbal directions are given. The graphics also give clear clues for what to do. Kids complete five activities and then win a "prize," which is an item they get to add to their virtual aquarium.

There are several different types of activities the child completes. For addition, subtraction and patterns, brightly colored numbers and shapes appear on the monkey's board. Kids solve the problem by dragging the correct answer into place. They get multiple-choice options supplied by cute crabs carrying the answers in sand buckets.

For connect-the-dots and tracing numbers, kids draw lines in the island "sand" using their finger. For number recognition, counting and learning the concepts of less and more, the monkey mascot blows "bubbles" and kids choose the correct answer by "popping" the bubble (which even makes a popping sound). For any of the activities, the monkey kindly lets kids know if they get a wrong answer.

What it Teaches/Develops:

This app teaches preschoolers fundamental math skills including number recognition, simple addition, subtraction, counting, patterns, shapes and number sequencing. All of the activities are intuitive, with verbal directions as needed, and easy enough to provide a high rate of success, which is important at this age level.

The Good:

All of the activities are great at teaching and reinforcing basic math concepts in a fun learning environment. Young kids will love the music and animation. The interactive component is perfect for the age level. Plus, collecting prizes for the aquarium is a neat twist. Not only does it provide a reward for success, but kids will like filling their tank and watching the tropical fish swim around!

The Bad:

The best part of the app for kids is winning prizes for the aquarium, but unfortunately the tank can get "full." When it does, the child has to remove some of the fish in order to add new ones. This can be pretty disappointing to a preschooler who has worked hard to win prizes and wants to see all of their fish, castles and treasure in the aquarium at once.

Additional:

With continuous, uninterrupted play your child will spend a lot of time with this app. They'll be able to navigate it on their own and won't need much, if any, direction on how to do the activities. They'll love getting the prizes for their aquarium and will be so proud of it, they'll want to show it off to you!

Monkey Preschool Lunchbox

Recommended Age Group: Preschool-Kindergarten

Grades:

- Educational—A-

- Fun— A-

- Overall— A-

Price: $0.99 (No free version)

Developer: THUP Games

Compatible: iPhone

Review

What it is:

For preschoolers learning basic concepts, "Monkey Preschool Lunchbox" is a fun, interactive app that will fully engage kids. Set against an island background with tropical music and a cute monkey mascot, your child will love playing this app again and again.

How it Works:

The app starts up quickly simply by touching "play." The first activity comes up on the screen and verbal directions are given. The graphics also give clear clues for what to do. Kids complete three activities and then win a "prize," which is a virtual "sticker" they get to put up on a board.

There are several different types of activities the child completes, all of which have to do with fruit. Each time they get the correct answer, the fruit goes into the monkey's lunchbox. For recognizing colors kids touch only the fruit of a certain color. For counting, kids touch the number of fruits indicated. For letters, kids pick the fruit that starts with that letter. For matching, kids have to find where the matching fruit are hidden and then remember where they are. For shapes and patterns, kids have to match fruit puzzle pieces to complete the fruit picture. For any of the activities, the monkey kindly lets kids know if they get a wrong answer.

When your child successfully completes three activities, they win a prize, which is an animated "sticker" they get to place anywhere on their sticker board. The stickers dance around and stay on the board for the duration of the app.

What it Teaches/Develops:

This app teaches preschoolers fundamental concepts such as colors, letters, counting, shapes, sizes, matching and grouping. All of the activities are intuitive, with verbal directions as needed, and easy enough to provide a high rate of success, which is important at this age level.

The Good:

The app offers a variety of activities that reinforce basic concepts, are appropriate for the age level and fun for young kids to do. The music and animation are lively and entertaining, and having all of the answers as "fruit" that goes into the monkey's lunchbox is a great idea that really appeals to young kids. The animated stickers as rewards are also a fun addition. Kids love choosing from a variety of characters to place wherever they want on the sticker board, and the stickers shake, bob and wiggle to the music.

The Bad:

A few times after placing the stickers on the board, the game stuck and didn't automatically return to the activities. Also, if your child exits out of the app, they will lose all the stickers they had accumulated on the board.

Additional:

This app offers unlimited play with continual activities and rewards. The simple concepts and easy-to-follow directions are perfect for preschoolers. The animated stickers are cute and a good reward program. Kids will have fun playing this app and learning at the same time!

TeachMe: Kindergarten

Recommended Age Group: Preschool-Kindergarten

Grades:

- Educational--A

- Fun—B

- Overall—A-

Price: $0.99 (No free version)

Developer: 24x7digital LLC

Compatible: iPhone

Review

What it is:

To help children learn basic Kindergarten skills, "TeachMe: Kindergarten" uses a cute, friendly mouse as the teacher to review subjects such as simple addition, subtraction, spelling and sight words.

How it Works:

Parents can select the subject area then touch "play" to start the questions. A mouse character in the upper right corner of the screen asks a question and gives instructions on how to answer. All answers are multiple choice. Touch the answer to select. If it's correct, the mouse gives positive feedback and a check mark at the bottom of the screen.

For every three check marks, kids earn a coin. Coins allow them to buy stickers and place them on various colorful scenes.

The app allows for parent controls using a password.

What it Teaches/Develops:

This app reinforces a number of basic Kindergarten skills, including simple math, spelling and sight words. The multiple choice options help kids have a higher degree of success, and the reward system provides positive reinforcement.

The Good:

This app is an excellent educational tool. It is fun, engaging, and encourages kids to improve with each series of questions. The more they play, the more coins they earn, and buying as many stickers as they can is a fun reward. Parents can also review scores and compare up to four children at once.

The Bad:

It may take a little time to learn how the rewards work and how to pay for a sticker, but parents can certainly guide their children.

Additional:

This is a fun, educational tool parents can use to help prepare their child for Kindergarten. They can also upgrade with an in-app purchase for $1.99 that increases the number of children that can be tracked at once. This would be a great way for teachers to assess individual students.

Creative Arts

Creativity through art, music and pretend play.

Cookie Doodle

Recommended Age Group: Preschool-Kindergarten

Grades:

- Educational—B+

- Fun—B+

- Overall—B+

Price: $0.99 (No free version)

Developer: Shoe the Goose

Compatible: iPhone

Review

What it is:

Baking with kids can get messy, but "Cookie Doodle" handles all the mess so kids can just have fun. This app lets them add all the ingredients into the bowl, stir it up, roll out the dough, bake any cookie shape they want and then decorate it. At the end they can even eat it!

How it Works:

To get started, kids can choose to use one of 21 "instant" doughs or choose from 24 "make your own" dough recipes. If they choose to make their own, a large mixing bowl comes up in the middle of the screen. The ingredients are listed on the side and graphics of each ingredient sit around the bowl. Drag each ingredient into the bowl. All of them have their own interactive component. For example, tilt the iPad to pour in the vanilla.

After the dough is mixed, "roll" it out with the rolling pin. Then choose a cookie cutter from the menu of more than 200 shapes. "Cut out" the cookie then touch the oven button to "bake it." When it's done, there are a variety of options for decorating. These include choosing a color of frosting and adding piping, 60 different sprinkles and 85 different candies.

Once the cookie is complete, kids can take a picture of it to keep, put it on a plate and save it for later or eat it. If they eat it, there is a prize waiting at the end.

There are some customizable options, including turning the sound off or on and choosing which decorations to include.

What it Teaches/Develops:

This is a good app that simulates following directions to make a recipe in a step-by-step process. It promotes creativity and allows kids to engage in their own type of pretend play, which is an important social and emotional development milestone for these age groups.

The Good:

This is a really creative app that both boys and girls will really enjoy. It simulates every step of the baking process, but lets kids experiment in a safe environment. The interactive component is really good with lots of fun animation. "Cracking" the egg, "stirring" the ingredients and "pouring" the vanilla are all great actions. There are a lot of decorating options that kids can choose, and the accompanying sound effects enhance the experience.

The Bad:

There aren't any verbal instructions and younger children may need some help reading the written directions. However, most of the interaction is intuitive so children will be able to navigate it on their own.

Additional:

This app really let's kids be creative and have some fun. Once they discover how many different kinds of cookies they can bake, they'll want to make dozens and dozens. Luckily, they won't get a tummy ache after eating any of these cookies!

Color and Draw Kids HD: 4 apps in 1

Recommended Age Group: Preschool-Kindergarten

Grades:

- Educational—A

- Fun—A

- Overall—A

Price: $1.99 (No free version)

Developer: Tipitap Inc.

Compatible: Not with iPhone

Review

What it is:

For kids who love to color, draw and decorate pictures, "Color and Draw for Kids HD: 4 apps in 1 Coloring Book" is a very advanced program. With options to draw freehand, color in pictures, decorate photos and practice writing the letters and numbers, every kid will enjoy being creative with this app.

How it Works:

From the main menu, choose from a variety of coloring options, including using a white canvas, black canvas, textured background, coloring page or lined paper for practicing writing letters and numbers. After choosing an activity, a full screen "easel" comes up. A bar of scrolling colors is at the bottom along with all of the tools.

Under the "brushes" setting, kids can choose from a pencil, spray can, paint bucket and shapes. They can also choose the thickness of the lines and the transparency. There is also an "erase" setting, "undo" setting and a "stickers" setting.

Kids simply touch a color to begin painting with their finger. For detailed work, there is a "zoom" button that increases the size of any section of the picture. There is also a voiceover that gives interactive instructions such as "draw a big bone in the dog's mouth."

Parents can upload actual photos to the app, and kids can add stickers or draw their own pictures on top of the photos. All of the drawings kids complete can be saved to the photo gallery.

The app does come with detailed written instructions under an additional menu, and some settings options for customizing the erase tool and voiceovers.

What it Teaches/Develops:

With this app children have the opportunity to practice their fine motor skills and tap into their creative artist. There are so many options for kids to explore, whether it's simply coloring in a picture, adding their own drawings to it, experimenting with backgrounds and textures or practicing writing letters, numbers or their own words.

The Good:

The coloring and drawing options with this app are limitless. The program provides 50 coloring pages that appeal to this age group, as well as stickers. There is a large range of bright colors to paint with and many drawing tools for kids to explore.

The best part of this app is how realistic the touch-screen drawing capability is. Other drawing apps either fill in the shape when kids touch it, or the strokes are blocky. With this program, kids can get very detailed with their coloring and have a true interactive drawing experience.

The Bad:

For younger children, parents may have to show their kids all of the options and settings for working with the drawing and coloring tools, but once kids have the hang of it, they will easily be able to navigate on their own.

Additional:

With the variety of drawing options, including the lined paper for practicing writing, and the high quality of the drawing capabilities, this is one of the best drawing apps available for kids in the preschool and kindergarten age groups.

iPaint Kids

Recommended Age Group: Preschool-Kindergarten

Grades:

- Educational--B

- Fun—B

- Overall—B

Price: $2.99 (Free version available)

Developer: Siro Barbera Abril S.L.

Compatible: Not with iPhone

Review

What it is:

Coloring is a favorite activity for preschoolers, and "iPaint Kids" is an app that turns your iPad into a big coloring book. With easy-to-use tools, bright colors and fun images, kids will have lots of pictures to hang on the digital bulletin board.

How it Works:

The app comes preloaded with images to color or parents can download their own from the iPad's photo album. To color one of the 11 preloaded images simply select "Draw" and touch any of the images.

The app provides many different coloring tools. These include a range of brushes, colors, and fun shapes. There is even an option to auto-color sections of the image that is helpful for younger kids. When your child is done, the colored page can be saved to the photo album.

To color a downloaded image, select "Import Image" and choose a picture from the photo album. Pictures that are black and white drawings or solid color images work better with the painting program.

What it Teaches/Develops:

This app helps develop a child's creativity and self-expression through art. It allows for limitless possibilities and combinations that will keep kids engaged.

The Good:

The app has vibrant colors, appealing images and fun tools for small kids. It's easy for little fingers to navigate and the coloring mechanism is simple. Being able to download additional images is a nice feature for parents to use.

The Bad:

The app does not provide any directions on how it operates. It may take a little time to experiment with the app to learn how everything works.

Importing images into the app is a little tricky. It may take a long time to process the image and there are no on-screen messages that indicate if the image is being downloaded. It simply looks like the iPad is frozen.

Additional:

"iPaint Kids" is a simple coloring book app that includes many colors and painting options kids will enjoy. There is a free version parents can download if they want to have their child test it out before purchasing this full version.

Kids Song Machine HD + 10 songs

Recommended Age Group: Preschool-Kindergarten

Grades:

- Educational--B
- Fun—A+
- Overall—A-

Price: $2.99 (Free version available)

Developer: Genera Kids

Compatible: Not with iPhone

Review

What it is:

Learning classic children's songs like "Old MacDonald" is not only fun but also it's educational, and "Kids Song Machine HD + 10 songs" will help your child learn ten of the most popular ones. It's an entertaining app that lets kids sing along and read the words at the same time.

How it Works:

After launching the app kids are taken to a screen with a colorful song machine, complete with gears and pipes. Inside this song machine is an image that represents a song. There are 10 images that represent 10 popular children's songs, including "Old McDonald," "Itsy Bitsy Spider" and "Jingle Bells."

Select "Go" to start a song. For example, when your child selects the Green VW image, it leads to an animated, colorful scene with the green VW. A children's voiceover sings the Itsy Bitsy Spider while highlighted lyrics appear on the screen. The scenes are also interactive. Tap on the screen and a variety of animation takes place.

To get to a new song select "Push." The gears on the song machine move and stop on another image. This new image represents a new song. Push "Go!" to start the sing-along fun.

What it Teaches/Develops:

This app teaches kids the lyrics to 10 of the most classic children's songs. It also helps them begin to recognize words that are highlighted on the screen.

The Good:

This is a fun, lively and highly interactive app. It adds the lyrics to the song so children can learn to read the words. The addition of rich, colorful graphics and the animation will keep a child's interest for quite some time.

The Bad:

Since there is no information on how to use the app, it may take a little time for kids to figure out how to work the song machine.

Additional:

There is a free version available that only has one song, but kids will no doubt want the full version. This is a fun, captivating sing-along app, and children can spend hours exploring, playing and singing.

Kids Song Machine 2-Around the World

Recommended Age Group: Preschool-Kindergarten

Grades:

- Educational--B

- Fun—A+

- Overall—A-

Price: $2.99 (Free version available)

Developer: Genera Kids

Compatible: iPhone

Review

What it is:

Exploring music from other cultures is a great educational tool, and "Kids Song Machine 2-Around the World HD" provides kids with an opportunity to learn songs from other countries. It has eight songs that kids can learn the words and sing along with the music.

How it Works:

After launching the app kids are taken to a screen with a colorful song machine. Inside this song machine is an image that represents a song from a certain country. There are eight images that represent eight countries, such as the United Kingdom, China and the Alps. The corresponding songs are "London Bridges is Falling Down," "Under the Dragon," and "Yo de le hi ho!"

Select "Go" to start a song. For example, when your child selects the red, double-decker bus, it leads to an animated, colorful scene with the red, double-decker bus in London. A children's voiceover sings the London bridges song while highlighted lyrics appear on the screen. The scenes are also interactive. Tap on the screen and a variety of animation takes place.

To get to a new song select "Push." The gears on the song machine move and stop on another image. This new image represents a new song. Push "Go!" to start the sing-along fun.

What it Teaches/Develops:

This app is a good way to expose kids to songs from other countries and learn different sounds and song styles. They can learn the words, many of which will be new for them, and can sing along to the words on the screen.

The Good:

This is a fun, highly interactive app that uses songs and images that are popular in foreign countries. It adds the lyrics to the song so children can learn to read the words. The addition of rich, colorful graphics and the animation will keep a child's interest for quite some time.

The Bad:

Since there is no information on how to use the app, it may take a little time for kids to figure out how to work the song machine.

Additional:

There is a free version available that only has one song, but kids will no doubt want the full version. This is a fun, captivating sing-along app, and children can spend hours exploring, playing and singing.

Music Sparkles

Recommended Age Group: Preschool-Kindergarten

Grades:

- Educational—B

- Fun—B

- Overall—B

Price: Free (Full version in-app purchase $2.99)

Developer: Kids Games Club

Compatible: iPhone

Review

What it is:

For kids who to love to bang on the drums all day, "Music Sparkles—All in One musical instruments collection of Sound, Vocals and Fun Entertainment" will keep their hands busy. This app provides kids with virtual instruments that they can "play" and create their own music.

How it Works:

On the startup menu, there are three settings to choose from: the xylophone, drum set and vocal notes. For xylophone, a colorful, full screen xylophone comes up with two playing sticks. Touch a bar and it plays that note, creating an animated "sparkle" effect. The more kids play, the more the screen sparkles. There are also four different octaves the xylophone can play, and kids can experiment playing each of them.

The drum set is similar to the xylophone. For that setting, a full drum set comes on screen, again with two drumsticks. Each time kids touch a drum or cymbal, it plays and sparkles float across the screen.

For the vocal notes setting, a scale with notes appears on the screen. Touch a note, and a voice sings "do, re, mi, fa, sol, la, ti, do." Kids can make up their own songs, which the app sings to them.

For both the xylophone and drum set, there are five different music loop options to accompany the songs kids create. These include background music from a guitar, bongos, banjo, drums and piano.

What it Teaches/Develops:

This app will encourage kids to be creative and find their inner musician. It will help them practice rhythm and recognizing the tone and sounds of different instruments.

The Good:

This is an app that children of all ages can enjoy. The colors are bright, the sound is clear and the animation is fun. It's extremely simple, so kids with very little knowledge of music can still play. It also allows them to play as fast as and crazy as they like—the more times they kit the keys the more notes they create that move and "sparkle!"

The Bad:

It doesn't teach actual notes or give any helpful hints for how to actually play an instrument. It's exploratory only.

The free version of this app only includes the xylophone, drum set, and vocal notes. There are nine additional instruments that are available, but only through in-app purchase. These include classic guitar, electric guitar, harp, saxophone, recorder flute, grand piano, accordion, harmonica and pan flute. You can purchase the full version for $2.99, or select individual instruments for $0.99 each.

Additional:

Kids love musical instruments, and this app gives them a good platform for playing in a variety of ways and styles, especially with the full version that has all the extra instruments. No matter what your child's age, they can enjoy making their own music and songs in a fun, interactive environment that provides good entertainment.

Paint Sparkles Draw—my first colors HD

Recommended Age Group: Preschool-Kindergarten

Grades:

- Educational—A-

- Fun—A-

- Overall—A-

Price: Free (Full version in-app for $3.99)

Developer: Kids Games Club

Compatible: iPhone

Review

What it is:

Regardless of age, kids love to color, paint and draw, and "Paint Sparkles Draw—my first colors" let's children be as creative as they want. This is a fun app where kids can explore colors, textures and backgrounds and make a variety of pictures in a finger-painting style.

How it Works:

The app starts up with a blank, white full-screen "canvas." In the bottom right corner is a palette of 10 colors. Next to it are three other menu options; a trash can to delete pictures, an eraser to correct mistakes and an easel. Touch the easel and a full menu of drawing options come up. Kids can choose from seven different outlined coloring "sheets" with fun characters, or choose a solid-colored background of their choice.

This menu also gives options for drawing tools. There are three different sized paintbrushes, a paint bucket and a row of "pencils" with varying degrees of brightness. Kids can choose any combination of these to use. For younger kids, they can paint by filling in the large areas of the coloring pages simply by touching them. Older kids might prefer using their finger as a paintbrush to get more detailed drawings, allowing them to make their own creation.

Each time a color is chosen, a voiceover says the name of the color. Whenever a "color" is applied to the canvas, bright, animated "sparkles" float on the screen accompanied by a musical sound effect. There is also a menu option that allows kids to save their picture to the photo album folder on the iPad.

What it Teaches/Develops:

This app both teaches and reinforces learning colors for younger children, and encourages creativity and artistic expression in children of all ages. It also helps kids develop hand-eye coordination and fine motor skills.

The Good:

This is a fun drawing app with lots of bright colors and great animation. Kids can really be creative and make a variety of pictures. The navigation is fairly simple and it's an app that appeals to a wide variety of ages. The sparkles and sound effects really enhance the experience and bring something different for kids to enjoy.

The Bad:

At first glance, the menu options seem easy to navigate. However, the "pencils" are a little confusing. It seems like these are drawing tools, but they are really just different levels of brightness. The paintbrushes are the only actual drawing tools. Unfortunately there are no verbal directions for the app to help instruct what to do. It's similar with the erase tool, which can be a little confusing to navigate.

This is another app that requires in-app purchases in order to unlock additional coloring background options. The free version of the app only has seven coloring pages, but there are 140 additional pages available for purchase.

Additional:

For those kids interested in drawing, this is a fun app that small children will really enjoy. It provides a rich, dynamic experience, and no matter what kids make they will be successful in creating a picture that they can keep and be proud of.

TJs Art Studio

Recommended Age Group: Preschool-Kindergarten

Grades:

- Educational--A+

- Fun—A+

- Overall—A+

Price: $1.99 (No free version)

Developer: UmaChaka Media, Inc.

Compatible: Not with iPhone

Review

What it is:

"TJ's Art Studio" turns the iPad into a portable art studio for kids. It is a powerful yet easy-to-use art app that lets young children be creative using pencils, paintbrushes, stickers, numbers, letters, photographs and much more.

How it Works:

To use this app, the key is to learn how to use all the tools. The developer has made this simple by including five short, fun how-to videos. To find these videos, select the "i" button on the bottom of the main menu. The five videos will show kids how to use the drawing and painting tools, stickers, shapes, letters, numbers, backgrounds and the photo and art albums.

When the videos are finished, select "start" to begin creating. After a child finishes a picture they can save it and share with family and friends.

What it Teaches/Develops:

This app promotes creativity and self-expression through art. The tools are easy for young children to work with so they can truly do everything on their own without the assistance of an adult.

The Good:

This app is very easy for children to navigate. Even the video tutorials are easy for kids to understand. The characters in the app are appealing to kids, and there are a number of creative tools to use. Kids can draw with pencils, paint with brushes, add stickers, shapes, numbers and letters to their pictures. They can also add their own photographs. Once they're finished, they can email their creation to grandparents or other family members.

The Bad:

There is nothing bad about this app.

Additional:

For only $1.99 kids have access to all the tools and backgrounds they need to easily create fun, colorful pictures. It is a well thought out concept that provides a comprehensive set of art tools that kids can easily work with on their own.

Intellectual Reasoning

Activities that help develop problem-solving skills.

Handy Manny Workshop

Recommended Age Group: Preschool-Kindergarten

Grades:

- Educational--A

- Fun—A+

- Overall—A

Price: $0.99 (No free version)

Developer: Disney

Compatible: iPhone

Review

What it is:

For kids who love Disney's Handy Manny TV show, "Handy Manny's Workshop" will really keep them busy. The app is a collection of fun activities including finding hidden items, a matching game, coloring, and completing a puzzle.

How it Works:

The main menu lets kids choose from five activities: "Find it," "Match it," "Color it," "Puzzle it," and "sing it," which lets kids sing along with the popular Handy Manny theme song.

In the "Find it" activity kids must find all of the tools hidden Handy Manny's colorful workshop. In "Match it" kids play a traditional matching game and must remember the tools hidden behind each card on the screen. There are three levels: easy, hard, and harder.

In "Color it" kids select a color and fill in the picture on the screen using their finger as a painting tool. The pictures can be saved to the iPad's photo album. In "Puzzle it" kids drag puzzle pieces into the correct spaces to complete a picture. Again there are three levels: easy, hard, and harder.

What it Teaches/Develops:

This app reinforces a number of skills, including problem solving, memory, creativity with the songs and coloring and spatial reasoning with the puzzle activity.

The Good:

This is a high-quality app from Disney. It builds off the popular children's show to get kids involved with fun, educational activities. It has quality animation, music, sound and a variety of challenging games. It is easy to use and weaves in Spanish words into the games.

The Bad:

This is a great app with no downside.

Additional:

"Handy Manny Workshop" is an excellent, fun, and superior app that provides kids with many games that educate and entertain. Preschoolers will love playing with Handy Manny on the iPad.

Kindergarten-Elementary: 5-10 years old

Language & Literacy

Develop skills to help kids to read, write, listen, concentrate, increase their vocabulary and more.

Ansel & Clair's Adventures in Africa

Recommended Age Group: Kindergarten-Elementary

Grades:

- Educational—A-

- Fun—A-

- Overall—A-

Price: $4.99 (No free version)

Developer: Cognitive Kid, Inc.

Compatible: Not with iPhone

Review

What it is:

"Ansel & Clair's Adventures in Africa" is a fully animated, interactive story app that completely immerses children into an adventure to Africa. Whether it's learning about the weather conditions, matching animals to their skins, finding Egyptian treasure or taking photos for the log, kids can spend hours exploring the African continent.

How it Works:

The app starts up like a video game, with an individual player setting up their name. An animated introduction plays, which features Ansel, a friendly space photographer from the planet Virtoos, and Clair, a Virtoosian robot. Ansel explains that they are taking their spaceship, Marley, to study Africa. Once they land, kids have the option to choose which part of Africa they want to explore: the Nile, the Serengeti or the Sahara.

In each area, there are a number of activities. Click on any of the areas to learn about an animal, the land, or other interesting aspects of that area. A virtual camera allows kids to take pictures of any of the objects, which they then can arrange in their "log." Click on the light bulb button beside any item to learn more facts. There are also hidden games and puzzles to solve, such as matching animals to their skins and guiding Marley through a maze of pyramid tunnels (by tilting the iPad) in order to reach the mummy's treasure. Each game has three levels to pass: easy, medium and hard.

There are also parts of Marley's space ship scattered around each area, which can be found by clicking on certain items. At any time, touch the space ship to go to a new area that can be explored.

What it Teaches/Develops:

This app teaches kids on multiple levels. They must rely on their listening and comprehension skills when Clair is explaining about an animal or other aspect in an area. They must use their reading skills when finding out additional factual information. They are also getting a valuable geography lesson, not only in where Africa is located in the world, but also where each area of Africa is within the continent.

The Good:

This app is incredibly dynamic and has so many levels to explore. The concept is very appealing to this age group, especially with the video game like qualities. The animation and graphics are very good and there are many opportunities for interactive learning. The combination of narrative, games and activities is a good balance from a learning perspective.

The Bad:

The only downside to this app is that some of the narrative elements can be a little long for kids to listen to. They may want to touch a button and explore items quickly, rather than have to wait for the app to explain something. It's also not obvious where the games, puzzles and space ship parts are located. Kids must really spend some time with a page in order to discover these hidden aspects.

Additional:

This is an app that uses a number of tools to help kids learn about the African continent. It has unique content that kids can explore in a fully animated, interactive environment. It's fun, interesting and will keep older kids entertained and engaged in a variety of educational activities.

Recommended Age Group: Kindergarten-Elementary

Grades:

- Educational—A+

- Fun—A

- Overall—A+

Price: Free (Full version in-app for $6.99)

Developer: BrainPOP

Compatible: iPhone

Review

What it is:

For parents and teachers who want an app that can truly supplement school curriculum, "BrainPOP Featured Movie" will give them everything they need. Kids watch an entertaining, educational animated movie, and then take a quiz to test their knowledge.

How it Works:

The main menu shows a graphic of the free movie, which changes daily. Touch the "play" button to start the movie. It is a short, two to three minute animated movie that features two characters: Tim and his robot Moby. They discuss the topic of the day, such as "the Supreme Court." As Tim talks about different aspects, everything he says appears in subtitles at the bottom of the screen. At the end of the movie, kids can take a quiz to test their knowledge based on what they just watched. They can also keep and track their quiz scores.

There is a full range of subjects that are covered in this app. They include: science, social studies, English, math, arts and music, health and technology. In addition to the featured movie of the day, there is also an archive of free movies in each category that are available.

For additional subscription fees, parents can download four additional movies related to the day's topic, which is $1.99/month, or they can have access to more than 750 movies and quizzes for $6.99/month.

What it Teaches/Develops:

There is virtually no limit to what this app can teach. It covers all subjects and supplements a wide variety of school curriculums. It really emphasizes listening and comprehension. Kids must pay attention to the movie in order to successfully answer the questions for the quiz at the end.

The Good:

The animated movie is very good and features entertaining characters. The material presented is easy to understand and appropriate for a wide variety of ages. The concept of featuring a new movie every day is creative, and offering an archive of additional movies in each category provides immediate, continued educational opportunities. This app is already being widely used in schools and can serve as a great study tool and help kids with at-home assignments.

The Bad:

This app is completely focused on education and doesn't have a gaming component to it. The only downside of this is that kids may not elect to play with it unless they need it for a class or to help them with homework.

Additional:

BrainPOP has taken a web-based application and successfully applied it to mobile devices. This app combines traditional learning methods into a fully interactive program that teachers can use in the classroom and then kids can use on their own at home.

Burger Shop-Monster Planet HD

Recommended Age Group: Kindergarten-Elementary

Grades:

- Educational--B

- Fun—B+

- Overall—B

Price: $2.99

Developer: Summit Applications Corporation

Compatible: Not with iPhone

Review

What it is:

Order up! Kids can test their skills at making monster customers happy in "Burger Shop-Monster Planet." As each alien comes in the restaurant, children must make burgers and drinks to order. But if they're too slow, then they lose points for unhappy monster customers.

How it Works:

After touching "play" from the main menu a full screen space restaurant appears. An alien walks in and orders a burger, which is displayed as image above its head. In the middle of the screen is the food prep station. Tap each ingredient in the right order to make the burger on the plate then "serve" it up by dragging it to the customer. A drink order appears next. Fill the glass with the correct drink then serve that as well. New monsters continue to walk in with different orders.

Each monster has a visual timer and kids must serve the food and drinks before the time runs out. If they don't, then the monster walks away unhappy and kids lose points. If an order is incorrect, it has to be thrown away and points are lost again. However, if all monsters leave satisfied, then the level is complete. There are a total of 48 levels, and each one becomes harder with more customers and trickier orders to make.

What it Teaches/Develops:

Kids must be able to multitask in this game and concentrate on completing several orders at once. It also tests memory as kids must recall what each order is and correctly assemble it. The timed component really challenges kids and forces them to be able to react quickly.

The Good:

The graphics are really fun in this app with humorous monsters and a very colorful burger shop. There's catchy music that plays in the background and realistic sound effects, such as a door chime every time a new customer walks in. The game concept is unique, and there is a lot for kids to do and keep them engaged. The increased complexity with skill levels will motivate kids to continue playing to see how fast they can build burgers.

The Bad:

The app only encourages concentration and memory skills.

Additional:

There is a lite version of this app available for free, but the full version will keep kids engaged longer and provide more challenges for them.

Chicktionary for iPad

Recommended Age Group: Kindergarten-Elementary

Grades:

- Educational--A
- Fun—A-
- Overall—A

Price: Free (In-app purchases for $0.99 each)

Developer: Blockdot, Inc.

Compatible: iPhone version for $1.99

Review

What it is:

If parents are looking for a fun version of scrabble for their kids, then "Chicktionary for the iPad" is a great one to try. In this app kids must see how many words they can make out of a set of letters that are on the "hens" in order to complete all the "egg" words in the carton.

How it Works:

After selecting "play" kids can choose from two levels of play: timed and un-timed. In the timed activity, kids have three minutes to make as many words as possible out of the letters given. Simply touch a hen and its letter will move to the bottom of the screen. A green "word" button lights up if it's a correct word. Press "enter" and the word moves to the egg carton.

If kids get stuck, they can shake the iPad to rearrange the hens and see the letters in a different order. They can also select to have hints shown, which gives one letter of each possible word in the carton. They can also select a word to see its definition.

For the un-timed activity, kids can take as much time as they want trying to solve the entire word puzzle. There are points for every word and even hidden point prizes. Each set of letters can make 3, 4, and 5+ letter words. If kids don't finish a puzzle, they can save it and come back to it later.

What it Teaches/Develops:

This is a great app for teaching kids how to spell and improve their vocabulary, especially with the built-in word definition button. It helps them focus on letter and word patterns and encourages them to think quickly to complete a puzzle.

The Good:

This is a really creative activity with lots of good animation and graphics. The sound of hens "clucking" makes it especially dynamic. It's highly educational for kids, and they will enjoy being challenged, especially with the timed activity. They can even compete against their parents to see who can create the most words.

The Bad:

Not all kids will enjoy playing this app. Those who find spelling difficult or have a limited vocabulary could become easily frustrated. These children would benefit from taking their time and playing the un-timed activity.

Additional:

Only one set of puzzles is available with the free version, however there are in-app puzzle packs for $0.99 each. This is such a fun game, parents will want to consider the full version for those kids who really want to be challenged.

PrepositionBuilder

Recommended Age Group: Kindergarten-Elementary

Grades:

- Educational--B

- Fun—B

- Overall—B

Price: $9.99

Developer: Mobile Education Tools

Compatible: Not with iPhone

Review

What it is:

Parts of speech can be a tricky concept for elementary aged kids, but "PrepositionBuilder" helps them learn the nuances of using prepositions by providing them with easy to understand contexts and sentences a well as bright, colorful graphics.

How it Works:

To start the app, kids create their own profile and have the option to turn on or off audio instructions, correct answer reinforcement and having correct answer recorded. A video tutorial is also available at the bottom of the screen along with an information button describing prepositions and a settings button.

There are nine preposition modules to choose from. Each problem displays a picture and a sentence with a blank where the preposition should be. Below the picture are three word choices. Drag and drop the correct word into the blanks space to complete the sentence. If the answer is wrong, it displays another picture for additional help.

Once the correct sentence is completed, touch the button to advance to the next problem. After completing a whole set of sentences correctly, kids "unlock" part of a fun animated story. After 11 sets they get to see the entire story, which involves a pirate fishing on a boat.

What it Teaches/Develops:

This app focuses solely on prepositions, which is one of the more difficult parts of speech for kids to grasp. They learn the function of a preposition, which is to show relationships, usually linking nouns and pronouns or sentence clauses, and how the placement of the preposition can change the meaning of a sentence. Kids do need to pay attention to the pictures and understand the sentences in this app in order to make the correct word choice. It can be easy to choose the wrong one.

The Good:

The app will record the child's stats and archive them, which is a great tool for teachers and parents who teach at home. The educational value of this app is wonderful. Not many educational apps focus solely on one element like this one does.

The Bad:

The main menu is somewhat cluttered and a little overwhelming at first, but it prevents parents from having to search for all of the features. The one setting that is not easily accessible is the animation. It's only found under the "Show My Animations" button. This reward component is a great part of the app, but it's difficult for kids to find.

Additional:

For parents who really want to help their kids learn the often-difficult concept of prepositions, this is a great app that they will enjoy doing. It's a good addition to the educational apps in your iPad library.

Word Seek HD

Recommended Age Group: Kindergarten-Elementary

Grades:

- Educational—A-

- Fun—B+

- Overall—A-

Price: $.99

Developer: Idealix, Inc.

Compatible: Not with iPhone

Review

What it is:

Word searches are a common activity found in the classroom, and kids can practice at home with "Word Seek HD." Using a simple grid, kids connect the letters with their fingers to find as many words as possible within the time given.

How it Works:

After selecting "play" from the main menu, a full screen grid with bright green letter tiles comes up. Kids can choose either the standard 4x4 grid or the more challenging 5x5 grid. They then have three minutes to find as many words as possible using the letters on the grid. To complete a word, kids touch a letter then drag their finger in any direction to the next letter in the word, which must be connected to the previous letter. The app scores each correct word found and lists it in a box on the side of the screen.

If there are still words left at the end of the game, the app shows the complete list possible. Kids have the option to play the same board again or try a new board. They can also adjust the time setting and even play against other online users via the game center.

What it Teaches/Develops:

This app will help elementary aged kids with both spelling and vocabulary. It also challenges them to look at letters in a new way and think about how words are structured. It takes the traditional word search activity and turns it into a modern, interactive educational tool.

The Good:

The graphics on this app are extremely good and the navigation is simple. It's easy to drag and release the letters to form the words. The optional background music is also a nice feature. Even younger school aged kids will be able to play and find simple three-letter words while older kids can really test their skills with the 5x5 grid and faster time limit.

The Bad:

This is definitely geared towards older kids. There aren't any cute, colorful animal graphics or sounds. It's a challenging game, even for adults, and some kids may get frustrated and not enjoy it as much.

Additional:

For a real word search challenge "Word Seek HD" is a high-level activity. For kids who want to expand their vocabulary, this is a good activity they can try and even go up against their parents to see who scores higher.

Math

Teaches kids to add, subtract, multiply, divide, and to learn fractions.

Math (Math Racer)

Recommended Age Group: Kindergarten-Elementary

Grades:

- Educational--A

- Fun—B

- Overall—A-

Price: $3.99 (No free version)

Developer: i4software

Compatible: iPhone

Review

What it is:

Learning math facts is a critical skill for elementary students to learn, and "Math (Math Racer)" helps kids practice addition, subtraction, multiplication and division while trying to beat the clock. Kids can track results, play with friends, and work towards getting faster.

How it Works:

The app can be set up for any of the four math operations or with a mix of all of them. The number of questions can be selected as well, either 10, 20, 50 or 100 questions. A blackboard appears on the screen with a problem, such as "$9+3$." Each math problem gives four multiple-choice answers, such as "12, 13, 14, 27."

A timer appears at the top of the screen and times how quickly it takes your child to select the correct answer (by tapping on it). At the end, the app reveals how many answers were correct and the time taken to complete the quiz.

Following the quiz, a stats screen shows the number of right and wrong answers. Kids can then choose to repeat the quiz and view high scores.

What it Teaches/Develops:

This app helps to teach children how to add, subtract, multiply and divide. The timed element helps prepare kids for the type of timed tests administered in the classroom.

The Good:

This app turns the often-mundane skill of practicing math facts into a challenging game. It encourages kids to improve by tracking their scores. The timed element motivates kids to complete the quizzes faster each time and beat their previous scores or even compete against friends and classmates.

The Bad:

Math can be difficult for some kids to learn. It would be nice to have the option to turn off the timer so that kids who may be struggling don't feel the extra pressure of having to perform with time constraints.

Additional:

"Math (Math Racer)" is a valuable educational tool that parents and teachers can use to give elementary students extra practice with math operations that simulates what they will experience in the classroom.

Math BINGO

Recommended Age Group: Kindergarten-Elementary

Grades:

- Educational--A

- Fun—A

- Overall—A

Price: $0.99 (No free version.)

Developer: ABCya.com

Compatible: iPhone

Review

What it is:

For a new twist on the classic game, "Math BINGO" lets kids search for answers to math equations on a virtual Bingo card. Once they get five in a row, they have Bingo!

How it Works:

Before playing Math BINGO, kids get to select their own avatar and the type of game: addition, subtraction, multiplication, division or a mix of all four. They can also select the difficulty level: easy, medium or hard.

Math BINGO is similar to the classic board game. In this app your child is shown a series of math equations at the top of the screen. The card is filled with numbers. Touch the space with the correct number and a Bingo Bug fills the space. Fill five spaces in a row vertically, horizontally or diagonally and the game says "BINGO."

One additional challenge to this game is that there can be more than one space with a correct answer. There is a timer on the screen so kids need to pick the answer that gets five Bingo Bugs in a row as fast as possible.

There is a score provided at the end of each game that is based on time needed to complete the game and the number of incorrect answers. In addition, when your child has a high score, the reward is a Bingo Bug. These Bingo Bugs are saved on another screen and kids can make them spin and twirl around.

The app has another game, "Bingo Bug Bungee." Kids pull down a bungee cord and release it to send the bugs flying and knock coins off a game board.

The app allows for up to five players and one guest. There is a scoreboard that tracks the top three scores for each type of math equation and level of difficulty.

What it Teaches/Develops:

"Math BINGO" teaches kids to add, subtract, divide and multiply. They must be able to solve the equations quickly and repeatedly.

The Good:

Kids love playing Bingo, and this is fun way for children to learn math. It uses the concept of Bingo Bugs to capture attention and interest in the math problems. Children can compete with friends or themselves for high scores and more Bingo Bugs.

The Bad:

The game does not provide children a way to review wrong answers after the game is done.

Additional:

This app is an excellent and fun way for children to learn how to add, subtract, divide and multiply. Using the traditional Bingo game, kids won't even realize they're solving math problems.

Math Evolve

Recommended Age Group: Kindergarten-Elementary

Grades:

- Educational--A+

- Fun—A+

- Overall—A+

Price: $0.99 (Free version available)

Developer: Zephyr Games

Compatible: iPhone

Review

What it is:

"Math Evolve" is a totally unique way for kids to learn how to add, subtract, multiply and divide. The app has superior graphics and sound, and successfully combines a fun storyline, math equations and an arcade game all into one.

How it Works:

To begin, select the math difficulty (easy-medium-hard), game difficulty (beginner/advanced/expert), and the math operations (add/subtract/multiply/divide). The storyline is that your child is an alien from another planet and is being sent to earth to learn, evolve, and return home to save the planet from destruction.

The arcade game involves numbers, equations, enemies and more. To learn math, the "alien" bumps into moving numbers to answer math questions, creates math problems from scratch and works backwards from an answer to create a math equation. There is instant feedback on the screen for correct/incorrect answers.

There is a practice mode where kids practice the arcade game and a player history that tracks overall statistics.

What it Teaches/Develops:

Math Evolve teaches kids how to add, subtract, multiply and divide by finding correct answers to math problems, creating math problems with the correct answers, and working back from a math answer to select the correct numbers to get to that answer. By completing all of these tasks, kids are fully engaging in a number of disciplines to learn math concepts in a variety of ways, which strengthens their math skill overall.

The Good:

Everything in this game is designed to breakthrough barriers of learning math by using a storyline about an alien from a distant planet and an arcade game. Kids are challenged to understand math at a deeper level as they create math problems and not just find a correct answer. The graphics and storyline approach of the app are superb as well.

The Bad:

The app does not provide a way for children to review their mistakes.

Additional:

"Math Evolve" is a revolutionary approach to learning math. The arcade game approach is highly engaging and goes way beyond basic math problem solving. There is a free version of this app that includes only the first two levels, while the full version comes complete with all twelve levels.

Math Puppy-Bingo Challenge Educational Fame for Kids HD

Recommended Age Group: Kindergarten-Elementary

Grades:

- Educational--B+

- Fun—B+

- Overall—B+

Price: $0.99 (Free version available)

Developer: Kids Games Club

Compatible: iPhone

What it is:

"Math Puppy" is a fun way for kids to learn how to add, subtract, multiply and divide. There are two types of math games--Bingo and challenge. Both of these games use puppy illustrations to make math more kid-friendly.

How it Works:

The main menu has two game options: "Math Bingo" and "Math Challenge." In "Math Bingo" select the type of math problem and the level of difficulty. These include addition, subtraction, multiplication, division and a mix of all four. The levels include easy, medium and hard.

Kids are shown a series of math equations at the top of the screen and must tap the correct answer on the Bingo card. A timer tracks how long it takes to answer the questions at the top of the screen.

A correct answer causes a math puppy to fill that space, a puppy on the screen to jump up and bark, and a voiceover to give a positive word for feedback. For wrong answers, an "x" marks the spot on the board. When a column or row is filled with math puppies, it is a Bingo! A score is provided at the end of the game along with a positive message.

The app keeps a "Bingo High score" which is found by selecting the stars icon in the upper right of the home screen.

For the "Math Challenge" kids are given problems with multiple answers. They must tap on the correct answer within the specified time limit. After selecting all of the correct answers, the game advances to a more challenging level. The app also has a "Math Calculator" for adding, subtracting, multiplying and dividing.

What it Teaches/Develops:

"Math BINGO" teaches children to add, subtract, divide and multiply. They must be able to solve the equations quickly and repeatedly.

The Good:

This is an easy-to-use app that helps kids learn math. The graphics are bright and the puppy illustrations will appeal to kids so it doesn't feel like they're solving math problems.

The Bad:

There is no way for children to review which questions they got right and wrong at the end of either game. And, the calculator is difficult to use as it only shows one number in the calculator's window. This means that kids have to recall the problem they are entering.

Additional:

"Math Puppy" is a fun way for children to learn how to add, subtract, multiply and divide. There is a free version of this app available, but it only includes subtraction equations.

Motion Math HD

Recommended Age Group: Kindergarten-Elementary

Grades:

- Educational--A+

- Fun—A+

- Overall—A+

Price: $2.99 (No free version)

Developer: Motion Math

Compatible: Not with iPhone

Review

What it is:

Learning fractions can be challenging, but "Motion Math" is a unique app that does it in a fun, entertaining way. The game teaches fractions in all forms, including numerator/denominator (1/2), percents (50%), decimals (.5), and pie charts. It also uses engaging tactics such as tilting the iPad to manipulate answers.

How it Works:

The game follows a star trying to return home from a far away galaxy. The star falls slowly from the sky. A fraction appears on the screen or inside the star and can be represented as a numerator over denominator, a percent, a decimal or pie chart. Tilt the iPad to direct the star to land on the number line where the fraction correctly belongs.

If the placement along the number line is correct, a different fraction comes up. After a few correct answers, the star zooms up to the next level for a more challenging version of the game.

If the answer is incorrect, the star bounces up to try again, and the app provides a hint. These hints become stronger after each miss, going from an arrow showing which direction to try again, to a vertical arrow showing exactly where the star should hit.

A score is given at the end of the game, and there is an option to choose the level of difficulty from beginner to medium to hard.

What it Teaches/Develops:

This app teaches kids fractions in all its different forms by using motion and fun game play. Kids are exposed to a large number of concepts and given multiple opportunities to find the correct answer.

The Good:

This is a great concept for teaching kids fractions in a variety of forms. Using the tilting mechanism of the iPad is a great way to engage kids so they play an active role in finding the correct answers. It is age appropriate and provides kids with different levels of challenging problems to solve.

The Bad:

There is nothing bad about this app.

Additional:

"Motion Math" turns learning fractions into a fun experience for kids. They may spend hours with this app, as they move from one level to the next, and continue to strive for higher scores.

Motion Math Zoom

Recommended Age Group: Kindergarten-Elementary

Grades:

- Educational—A-

- Fun—B+

- Overall—A-

Price: Free (Full version $3.99)

Developer: Motion Math

Compatible: iPhone

Review

What it is:

To help kids learn place value with numbers, "Motion Math Zoom" features an expandable number line, fun animal graphics and bubbles that kids have to pop with their finger. Add the timed challenge, and this app becomes a complete educational math tool.

How it Works:

Kids start at the "Intro" level with a basic number line. A bubble containing a number, such as "5" floats across the screen. Kids move the number line by scrolling it with their finger until they find the space where the number 5 belongs. "Pop" the bubble by touching it and the number drops to its correct position. Complete several in a row to advance to the next level.

Higher levels include larger numbers, all the way into the thousands. For these, kids can shrink the number line by pinching it with their fingers in order to move more quickly to a higher place value. They can also spread the number line out to get to smaller numbers.

In addition to whole numbers, there are levels for negative numbers and decimals. There is also a timed challenge that features a needle. The needle slowly moves toward the bubble with the number in it. Kids must find the place value for the number before the needle pops the bubble.

What it Teaches/Develops:

This app focuses on teaching kids place value along a number line. The higher levels help kids learn about more advanced concepts, such as negative numbers and decimals to the hundredth place, and the needle really challenges them to think quickly.

The Good:

This a good educational tool that tests kids on an important math concept. It's easy to navigate and if kids get stuck, visual clues and written instructions appear on screen to help them. Each type of number features colorful, unique animal graphics such as frogs, dogs, and dinosaurs. The accompanying sound effects are nice and the timed challenge is a good feature as well.

The Bad:

The free version of the app only comes with six levels, but there are 24 total with the full version for $3.99. While it is a good supplemental math lesson, unless kids really enjoy working with numbers, it might not be an activity they gravitate towards on their own.

Additional:

The app does keep track of your child's score and it's a good way to let kids practice working with a number line. It will help them "see" numbers in an engaging, interactive way.

Rocket Math

Recommended Age Group: Kindergarten-Elementary

Grades:

- Educational--B+

- Fun—B+

- Overall—B+

Price: Free (Full version $0.99)

Developer: Dan Russell-Pinson

Compatible: iPhone

Review

What it is:

Build a rocket, blast off into space and learn math facts all with "Rocket Math Free." This is a fun, educational app that helps kids with math equations, telling time, number and more.

How it Works:

From the main menu kids set up their player profile then begin building their rocket. They choose a body style and several parts using the predetermined amount of money. Once they run out of money, they must answer math problems to earn more. They choose the type of equations, which include addition, subtraction, multiplication and division, as well as the level of difficulty, easy, medium or hard.

Math problems are presented as multiple choice. Simply touch the correct answer. After answering a series of problems, money is earned to buy additional parts. Answer all of them correctly, and kids get to spin a bonus wheel for extra money.

When the rocket is finished, kids can launch it into space and control the rocket's flight by tilting the iPad. To have a successful mission, kids need to answer additional questions about numbers, telling time, etc.

Based on the success of the mission, kids are awarded three medal types: a bronze, silver and gold.

What it Teaches/Develops:

This app teaches kids a range of topics including addition, subtraction, multiplication, division, telling time, US money, and shapes/patterns. It also lets them be creative with building their own rocket design.

The Good:

This is a good educational game that provides lots of interaction and excellent animation. It successfully combines a game component with a learning emphasis on math. The math problems are age appropriate and are good for a wide range of skill levels.

The Bad:

It takes a little time to learn how to play despite the instructions available in the app.

Additional:

This is a really good, free app that kids will enjoy and feel like they are just doing more math problems. There is a full version available for $0.99 that includes 56 different math missions.

TeachMe: 1st Grade

Recommended Age Group: Kindergarten-Elementary

Grades:

- Educational--A+

- Fun—A

- Overall—A

Price: $0.99 (No free version)

Developer: 24x7digitalLLC

Compatible: iPhone

Review

What it is:

"TeachMe: 1st Grade" is an app aimed at helping children in first grade learn four topics: addition, subtraction, spelling and sight words. It is highly interactive with a mouse as instructor, a Teach Town where children learn in the school and earn coins to have fun in the Shape, Fish and Art stores.

How it Works:

Parents can select the subject area then touch "play." After kids enter the school, a mouse character in the upper right corner of the screen asks a question and gives instructions on how to answer. Kids either tap on the correct answer to write it with their finger on the screen. If it's correct, the mouse gives positive feedback and a check mark at the bottom of the screen. If at any time your child needs help, the mouse provides it.

For every three check marks, kids earn a coin. Coins allow them to buy stickers from the Art Store, fish from the Fish Store and stretchable shapes kids can play with from the Shapes Store.

What it Teaches/Develops:

This app reinforces a number of basic first grade skills, including math, spelling and sight words. Being able to write in your own answers simulates a school environment, and the reward system provides positive reinforcement.

The Good:

This is an excellent educational tool with superior interactive help from the mouse/instructor. The app is able to read the answers your child writes on the screen. The Teach Town provides an added dimension of fun as children learn, earn, and buy rewards. Parents can easily review the progress of their children as well.

The Bad:

It may take a little time to understand how the stretchable shapes work in the Shape Store.

Additional:

This is a fun, educational tool parents can use to help supplement what their child is learning in first grade. They can also upgrade with an in-app purchase for $1.99 that increases the number of children that can be tracked at once. This would be a great way for teachers to assess individual students.

Creative Arts

Kids learn to draw, design, play music and create a story.

Create A Car

Recommended Age Group: Kindergarten-Elementary

Grades:

- Educational--B

- Fun—A-

- Overall—B+

Price: $0.99 (No free version)

Developer: ABCya.com

Compatible: iPhone

Review

What it is:

Little engineers will really enjoy getting creative with "Create a Car." This is a fun app that encourages children to use their imagination to build a car. There are wheels, engines, power tools and more to design a car. When a car is complete, your child can start it up.

How it Works:

At the beginning of the app, kids get to choose from more than 30 body styles for their car. Then they begin selecting parts to add to the car. There are more than 65 custom vehicle parts including different tire designs, decals, exhaust pipes, satellite dishes and tank treads. All of these parts are sizable and can be positioned anywhere on the vehicle as well as flipped or rotated. Simply touch and drag the parts to the car on the screen.

Once the car is complete, your child can start it up and watch the parts move. Cars can be stored in the garage and edited later. Kids can also create custom information for each vehicle. The car design can be shared with a friend via email.

What it Teaches/Develops:

This app encourages creativity in kids as well as helping them to work with proportions and making parts fit together neatly on the car.

The Good:

The app is fun and filled with great choices for all of the car parts. There are an unlimited number of car creations from mixing and matching parts. The car colors and the vehicle parts are bright and very unique. The app is also appropriate for both boys and girls.

The Bad:

It takes a little time to learn how all of the different vehicle parts are used on a car.

Additional:

This app is ultimately about encouraging children to be creative. Kids can design countless cars, and for those who are car enthusiasts, they will definitely want to spend the time designing their ultimate dream machine.

How to Draw—Easy Drawing Lessons

Recommended Age Group: Kindergarten-Elementary

Grades:

- Educational--A-

- Fun—B+

- Overall—A-

Price: Free (Additional in-app products starting at $0.99 each.)

Developer: ArtelPlus

Compatible: iPhone

Review

What it is:

For young artists who like to draw, "How to Draw— Easy Drawing Lessons" can provide them with some good practice. Using step-by-step instructions, kids can practice drawing a variety of pictures on screen, and then try them on their own later using actual paper.

How it Works:

The main menu shows a number of images and how many steps it takes to draw each one. Click on a picture and it brings it up on a screen with grid lines. There are three drawing modes. "A" let's kids try to draw the picture on their own. "B" shows what lines to draw in each step and "A + B" lets kids draw on top of the instruction lines, then erase the extra lines at the end.

The bottom of the screen displays all of the tool icons for drawing, painting, color palette, erasing and saving. To draw, simply touch the screen and either draw freehand or trace the red lines provided in each step then color in the picture.

The app comes with nine different pictures to draw. Additional pictures are available to download for free, and there are others available as in-app purchases.

What it Teaches/Develops:

This app will help kids learn to draw a number of different pictures in an illustration style. They can either try to replicate one of the pictures that comes with the app, or they can explore drawing on their own to develop creativity and express themselves freely.

The Good:

This is a great idea for older kids who are really interested in learning about beginning drawing. They can practice proper proportion and the gridlines on the screen make it easier to do that. There are a variety of pictures to draw, including animals and objects, and they are bright, fun graphics that would appeal to kids.

The Bad:

There aren't any written or verbal instructions for this app, and a lot of kids won't know how it works unless they spend some time experimenting with it. Many of the pictures require small, fine lines that can be difficult for kids to do using their finger on a touch screen. Given the large number of steps and the difficulty of some of the pictures, unless a child is really interested in learning to draw, some may not have the patience to spend with this app.

Additional:

This is a good free app for kids who really enjoy drawing. And for those who are ready to try more challenging pictures, there are in-app purchases available that include princesses, dinosaurs, Batman and sports cars.

How to Draw (Free Lessons)

Recommended Age Group: Kindergarten-Elementary

Grades:

- Educational--A

- Fun—B+

- Overall—A-

Price: Free (Full version $1.99)

Developer: Pacific Spirit Media

Compatible: iPhone

Review

What it is:

If your child loves to draw but doesn't want to take formal lesson, "How to Draw (Free Lessons) is a great app that can help teach them. It's a collection of 18 high-quality YouTube video tutorials for drawing faces, people, cartoons, scenes and shading techniques.

How it Works:

There are a variety of videos to choose from off the main menu. Simply select a topic and a video pops up within the app that shows a tutorial. Different instructors teach them, and if your child likes a particular teacher, they can click on links for other videos by that same teacher.

Some of the videos cover pencil drawing techniques, drawing with perspective, drawing faces, eyes, bodies, graffiti, flowers, and even 3D letters. All of the lessons focus on drawing with pencil.

What it Teaches/Develops:

This app covers a wide range of drawing techniques, concepts and helpful tips. Kids can follow the tutorials or they can try and draw different things on their own based on what they learn from the videos.

The Good:

The app is an easy way for children to access expert, high-quality video tutorials on how to draw. There are so many videos on YouTube, it can take a lot of effort to find the ones that are best. This app bundles the best ones so they are all in a single location. Interested kids can explore a wide variety of drawing videos and can focus on those techniques they enjoy the most.

The Bad:

When a child selects a link for additional videos from a given teacher, it takes kids to YouTube. Being outside the app, there is the potential for kids to access inappropriate material. There is also a banner ad that runs on the main screen of the app which links to outside content as well.

Additional:

This app is a fast way for children to access quality videos on how to draw. And for kids who want to expand their talents, there is even more content available when they link to a particular instructor's channel on YouTube.

Kids Music Maker HD

Recommended Age Group: Kindergarten-Elementary

Grades:

- Educational--A

- Fun—A

- Overall—A

Price: $1.99 (Free version available)

Developer: Genera Kids

Compatible: Not with iPhone

Review

What it is:

Exposing kids to different musical instrument styles is a great opportunity, and "Kids Music Maker HD" is a fun way to introduce musical notes and to encourage kids to play a number of popular children's songs.

How it Works:

From the main menu simply tap on one of six instruments shown in a bright, colorful scene--harmonica, xylophone, harp, flute, accordion, or piano. The rabbit hops down a purple path and when it reaches the instrument selected, a new screen appears.

On this new screen, there are six icons that represent six popular children's songs: "The Wheels on the Bus," "Hickory Dickory Dock," "Row Row Row Your Boat," "Itsy Bitsy Spider," "I'm a Little Teapot"" and Pat a Cake." Select one of these songs and touch the play button to begin the music.

A child's voiceover sings the song while the musical notes Do, Re, Mi, Fa, So, La, Ti and Do are highlighted in sync with the melody of the song. Animated graphics move with the notes and the song plays repeatedly.

There are also three buttons the child can explore. The "DoReMi" button encourages children to play the song using the musical notes. Each note of the melody lights up in order so kids know when to play them. The "Musical note" button automatically plays the entire melody by lighting up each note in order. The "Rabbit" button repeats the introductory screen where the voiceover sings the song.

What it Teaches/Develops:

This app introduces kids to musical notes, the sound and style of different instruments and encourages kids to play songs. The repetition helps them become familiar with the tunes so they can improve as they play.

The Good:

This is a fun way to introduce children to musical notes and playing an instrument. The graphics are colorful, there is a lot of animation, and there is a lot of content to explore. Kids will have fun and want to play their favorite songs over and over again.

The Bad:

There aren't any verbal or visual instructions with this app. Without parental assistance, kids may have problems navigating through the different activities.

Additional:

"Kids Music Maker HD" is a fun way to introduce children to music and encourage them play popular kids songs and even sing along. There is a free version of this app available for parents who want to test it out before purchasing this full version.

StoryBuilder for iPad

Recommended Age Group: Kindergarten-Elementary

Grades:

- Educational--A

- Fun—A-

- Overall—A

Price: $7.99 (No free version)

Developer: Mobile Education Tools

Compatible: iPhone version for $5.99

Review

What it is:

Children of all ages love to tell stories, and "StoryBuilder for iPad" lets them tell a story and record it in their own voice. Using a series of questions about pictures on the screen as prompts, kids get to decide what happens first, next and last.

How it Works:

There are several features to set up from the settings menu. Kids can enter their name and select the level of play. Level 1 is the easiest and displays question prompts related to what kids see on the screen. Level 2 requires kids to infer what could have happened before the picture on the screen and what might happen after. Level 3 lets kids tell a story without any prompts at all.

There are more than 50 story lines and 500 audio clips with the app. An image comes up on the screen and a voiceover asks a question such as "What happened?" There is text along the top of the screen that reads "But all of a sudden." Kids press "record" and read the text then add their own details about what happened based on the image they see. They can touch "play answer" to hear what they recorded. They can re-record as many times as they want, or touch "next question" to continue with the story.

Kids can also touch "repeat question" to hear it again. Once they have answered all the questions, they can hear the story in its entirety and in their own voice. They can also save the story in their own archive and play it again later or email it and share it with others.

What it Teaches/Develops:

This is an invaluable educational app that teaches kids how to formulate a story. It improves their creativity by thinking up new ideas and challenges their critical thinking skills by requiring them to infer what happens first, next and last. The auditory component helps them process the story based on what they hear.

The Good:

This is a great concept that kids across multiple ages will enjoy. Having three levels of play is good so that kids at different skill levels will be appropriately challenged. The story lines are fun and the graphics are engaging. Younger kids will be able to look at the pictures and answer questions about what happened, while older kids will have fun making up their own stories.

The Bad:

This is a higher priced app at $7.99, which may cause some parents to shy away from it. However, what it teaches is so important, and kids will enjoy making up their own stories and especially hearing them played back in their own voice.

Additional:

This app has been touted as a good tool to use for kids who have special needs such as autism spectrum disorders or sensory processing disorders because the use of audio clips promotes improved auditory processing.

Toontastic

Recommended Age Group: Kindergarten-Elementary

Grades:

- Educational--A

- Fun—A

- Overall—A

Price: Free (Additional in-app purchases starting at $0.99)

Developer: Launchpad Toys

Compatible: Not with iPhone

Review

What it is:

Kids love cartoons and now they can make their own with "Toontastic." This app provides a toolset for creating story-based cartoons including guides and colorful graphics. Kids are able to build their own scenes and even record their own voices then watch what they have created.

How it Works:

There is a parent's guide at the bottom of the main menu, which provides helpful instructions for all the options the app has.

The main menu has three buttons: Toy Store, ToonTube and Create Cartoon. Touch "Create Cartoon" and a voiceover gives verbal instructions on how to get started. Choose one of five scenes along the story arc: setup, conflict, challenge, climax and resolution. For each one, kids can choose the setting and characters either by drawing their own or selecting from the graphics provided.

Next touch the "start animation" button and begin moving the characters around the screen by dragging them. The app records the movements as well as any sounds/voices the kids make. When finished, click "stop animation" and the app replays all the sounds and movements.

Kids can share their cartoons with others using the ToonTube feature and can see other cartoons created by kids all around the world. The screen displays a globe with dots representing the location of where the videos were uploaded. Click on one and the bottom half of the screen provides the videos. There is also the option to search for cartoons by keyword, to see featured ones and to favorite some for returning to once you've registered and provide that access.

The Toy Store button features additional playsets, which are thematically collected elements to use in a story that are available for in-app purchases for $0.99 each. For example, the Supertastic Shinjuku Smackdown provides a children's version of a Godzilla scenario with a giant monster, a TV reporter, TV van and sushi.

What it Teaches/Develops:

Teaching children the elements of storytelling and allowing them to explore each concept is a vital tool. It lets kids be really creative and even develop their pretend play, which is an important developmental milestone.

The Good:

The privacy controls for both going on line and uploading are left strictly in the parent's hands. The graphics are also charming and every element has a distinct and powerful visual appeal to it. However, it's the creating a cartoon that is really special. There is a lot that goes into building each storyline, but there is a narrator that helps guide kids each step along the way.

The Bad:

The movement of the cartoon characters around the screen is not very fluid and can look somewhat awkward. However, there aren't many apps that allow kids to move graphics around the screen and then playback those movements.

The types of stories kids can tell are limited to only a few playsets with this version and kids will enjoy it so much they will want to purchase additional sets. However, the graphics are fun and appealing and the options that do come with the free version will keep them busy for quite a while.

Additional:

After downloading this version parents can register to receive a free playset by supplying an email address then activating the link provided. It's worth it to give your child even more tools for creating fun, interactive animated cartoons.

Social Studies

Facts about US Presidents, states, and weird but true facts.

Presidents vs. Aliens

Recommended Age Group: Kindergarten-Elementary

Grades:

- Educational—A-

- Fun—A-

- Overall—A-

Price: $0.99 (Free version available)

Developer: Dan Russell-Pinson

Compatible: iPhone

Review

What it is:

When it comes to an app that truly makes learning fun, "Presidents vs. Aliens" covers all the bases. In order to "knock down the aliens" kids must correctly answer questions about all 44 presidents of the United States. With surprise features, bonuses and adjustable skill levels, this is a great game that all school-aged kids can enjoy.

How it Works:

There are several ways to begin the game. For kids who want a bit of an advantage before playing, they can select the "learn" button, which provides important statistics about each of the presidents, including a headshot, the years they served, their affiliated party, their vice president, nickname, events they were involved in, quotes they said and other facts.

The other way to begin the game is by customizing a player under the "select player" button. There can be up to six unique players, each one with its own presidential or alien avatar and individual name. Once this step is complete, there is also the option to customize the type of questions asked. It can be as simple as "Identify President" or can include one or all of the following: "Political Party," "Before and After," "Historical Events," "Nicknames," "Quotes," and "Facts."

When setup is done, choose "Play Game." Full-screen images of historical presidential images appear, such as the White House, and small alien heads float on top. The question comes up at the top of the screen with four presidential headshots below it. For example, the question might ask, "Which of these presidents is Barrack Obama?" Touch the correct photo. If it's incorrect, the app shows you the correct answer and brings up a new question. If it's correct, then kids get the chance to "knock down" the aliens by aiming the president icon at the bottom of the screen and swiping their finger toward them. Once all of the aliens are gone, the level is completed.

If more than 60% of the answers are correct, then a random "president" is earned. When 15 presidents have been collected, then a new game is unlocked called "Heads of State," in which kids must identify the correct presidents that are floating in space. When 15 additional presidents are earned, a third game is unlocked called "Executive Order," in which all of the presidents must be arranged in the correct order they served.

The game becomes more difficult as obstacles surround the aliens, but additional features and bonuses pop up as well. For example, when certain questions are answered correctly, three president icons are won, or if the icon strikes a UFO, then it takes out additional aliens.

What it Teaches/Develops:

This app teaches kids a wide variety of facts about the presidents of the United States. It includes pictures of each president, their political party, predecessors and successors, their nicknames, quotes they said, historical events they participated in and general facts about them.

The Good:

This app has a lot going on with many things working in its favor. From an educational perspective it's a great way to teach kids historical facts that they might otherwise consider boring. It's a creative concept, and the video game type component will really keep kids engaged. The hidden features and bonuses keep it exciting and there are definite rewards for success, especially the additional games. The graphics and sound effects are fun, and there are a wide variety of settings to adjust for different ages and skill levels.

The Bad:

The combination of realistic presidential landmarks and cartoonish aliens is a little strange, but most kids will probably overlook it. However, they may lose patience with how long it can take to earn enough presidents to unlock the other games.

Unless kids really spend some time at the beginning studying the statistics for each president, much of what they do is going to be a guessing game. How much information they are actually retaining is somewhat questionable. And, younger kids may get frustrated if they don't have a lot of success. Even at the easiest level, identifying presidents from their picture might be too difficult.

Additional:

This app gets a lot of points for creativity and trying to make a fun game out of a social studies lesson. Kids will enjoy it, and parents can even get in on the fun. With the multiple player options, entire families can test their knowledge of the presidents against one another!

Stack the States Lite

Recommended Age Group: Kindergarten-Elementary

Grades:

- Educational--A+

- Fun—A+

- Overall—A+

Price: Free (Full version $0.99)

Developer: Dan Russell-Pinson

Compatible: iPhone

Review

What it is:

For a fun lesson in U.S. geography, "Stack the States Lite" is a good app to teach kids about all 50 states. They can learn the shape of the state, its location, capital, cities, landmarks and more.

How it Works:

The goal of this game is to build a stack of states (these are the shapes of the states) high enough to reach a checkered line, which is above a pedestal at the bottom of the screen.

Every correct answer to a geography question earns one state. Drop the state onto the pedestal and rotate it so it stacks upright and stays on the pedestal so the stack will clear the checkered line.

Once the stack is high enough to cross the line, the game ends. When a high enough percentage of questions are correctly answered, kids earn a reward. This is a state that is automatically placed on a map of the U.S. Continue to play the game until the entire map is complete.

What it Teaches/Develops:

This app teaches children about all aspects of U.S. geography as it pertains to all 50 of the states. It's structured in a fun game environment so that kids will be motivated to learn and remember important facts.

The Good:

The concept of "Stack the States Lite" is unique and a fun, challenging way for kids to learn about the 50 states. It does an excellent job of making learning about the U.S. geography engaging and entertaining for kids.

The states are personified with big eyes and react to being dropped above the pedestal and landing. Some even fall off the pedestal and disappear from the screen. It is a fun way to appeal to kids.

The Bad:

The instruction to tap the screen to start the game is somewhat confusing, and the free version does contain ads.

Additional:

This is an entertaining app with a high educational component. There is a full version for $0.99 that does not include ads and has an interactive map as well as additional games for kids to play.

WeirdButTrue

Recommended Age Group: Kindergarten-Elementary

Grades:

- Educational--B
- Fun—B+

- Overall—B

Price: $1.99 (No free version)

Developer: National Geographic Society

Compatible: iPhone

Review

What it is:

Kids love anything that is strange or funny, especially if it's true, so "WeirdButTrue" is a great app that will give them more than 300 interesting facts they can share with friends and family.

How it Works:

After starting the app "shake" or "swipe" the screen to bring up a fact. The facts can be presented with a visual, text, sound or a combination of all three. On the right column of each fact are icons. These allow kids to save the fact as a favorite, rate the fact on a meter, email the fact, and hear comments about the fact.

A plus icon opens up a menu screen that allows kids to review favorites, see the top weird facts chosen weekly by other users, search for facts, read instructions for the app, and get more information about National Geographic.

What it Teaches/Develops:

This app teaches kids more than 300 "weird but true" facts on a wide variety of topics including animals, weather, space and science. All of the facts are age-appropriate and entertaining to kids.

The Good:

All of the facts and trivia are kid-friendly and many will make them laugh. It's a great way for them to learn interesting pieces of information on a variety of topics, most of which children (and adults) won't already know. The rating meter is a fun feature, and kids can use the search feature to explore further. They can also share their favorites with friends.

The Bad:

Some parents may not want their kids "shaking" the iPad to change screens, but they can also bring up a new fact by swiping the screen.

Additional:

"WeirdButTrue" is a neat way to get kids interested in trivia about a wide variety of topics. It's fun, engaging and kids will enjoy learning facts about all things strange and unusual.

Additional Apps For:

Self-expression and emotional vocabulary, spatial reasoning & Telling time

Feel Electric!

Recommended Age Group: Kindergarten-Elementary

Grades:

- Educational—A+

- Fun—A+

- Overall—A+

Price: Free (No paid version)

Developer: Sesame Street

Compatible: iPhone

Review

What it is:

To help kids explore their emotions and have fun with words, "Feel Electric!" uses a number of engaging activities from "The Electric Company" TV show produced by Sesame Street. Kids can build their vocabulary while learning appropriate words to help express what they're feeling.

How it Works:

After the app launches a short video with a friendly face explains the activities. These include the menu items "My Life," "My Games," and "My Stuff." The first option, "My Life," has three activities. In "Mood Dude" kids tap on the character to change its facial expressions, body position and color to best reflect their own mood that day. In "Mood Tales" kids play a Mad Lib game where they choose words to create a funny story. In "Moodosphere" kids choose words that best describe their current emotions. If they don't know what a word means, simply tap on it to hear and see a definition.

The "My Games" option has three more activities. These are "Pets vs. Monsters," "Prankster Madness," and "Hey You Guys...Catch!" All of these fun games are interactive and kids must match the correct words to pictures of facial expressions.

The "My Stuff" option includes selections of photos, songs and videos all featuring The Electric Company kids. For every activity, clear directions are given both verbally and visually.

What it Teaches/Develops:

This app helps foster positive self-expression in children. Using a variety of fun activities, kids learn appropriate words for what they are feeling and how to properly communicate those feelings to others.

The Good:

This is a wonderful app that's really appealing to older kids. The subject matter is excellent, and the way it's presented is just as engaging and entertaining as The Electric Company TV series. There are a wide variety of activities, music and videos that all promote the concept of expressing emotions.

The Bad:

There is nothing negative about this app.

Additional:

This is a wonderful, free app that engages kids in fun activities that gives them the tools needed to learn how to express themselves in a healthy way. Parents can play with their kids and use the app as a platform for many discussions about feelings.

Pictorial HD

Recommended Age Group: Kindergarten-Elementary

Grades:

- Educational—A-

- Fun—A+

- Overall—A

Price: $1.99 (No free version)

Developer: Sergey Vasiliev

Compatible: iPhone

Review

What it is:

Elementary aged kids who like a challenge will love "Pictorial." This is a really creative app that takes the concept of identifying constellations in the night sky and turns it into a game of skill. The app incorporates interesting settings and backgrounds and even includes a few hidden secrets.

How it Works:

In the first level kids need to solve the "Night Town." Touch play from the main menu and a full screen graphic of a night sky above a neighborhood comes up. A cluster of white dots, or stars, is in the middle of the sky. A small image of a hand points where to start and dotted lines provide a guide to follow. As kids slide their finger across the screen, the constellation of stars move and begin to form a shape. Once the shape is aligned, the app signals that it's correct. Complete a number of pictures in a row, and a new level is unlocked.

There are five different levels, each with 30 different pictures to solve. In addition to "Night Town," there is "Arctic," which includes graphics of a snowy arctic night, complete with the Northern Lights. There is "Treasure Island" that has a treasure map background. There is the "Fairy Wood" with magical creatures and there is the "Halloween" level with a spooky night sky and witch's cauldron.

When the first cluster of stars appears on the screen, a small counter begins counting down in the bottom right corner. This represents the number of points given for completing a picture. The faster the picture is solved, the more points given. If the picture is not solved after several seconds, a help button appears. Touch this and the constellation slowly transforms into the completed picture, and then goes back to where it was so the child can finish solving it.

Each level incorporates bright graphics and backgrounds, pleasing music and simple animation that really add to the overall experience of the game.

What it Teaches/Develops:

This app is great for helping kids improve their spatial reasoning skills. They must be able to quickly visualize what the picture is supposed to be and then manipulate it in order to place the cluster of stars in the right place.

The Good:

This is a really unique app that offers elementary kids a great challenge. The graphics are compelling and appeal to both boys and girls, and there are a wide variety of pictures to solve. There are even two levels of difficulty, and kids can choose which level they are comfortable trying. The timed scoring adds an element of challenge, and unlocking a new level each time kids successfully complete a round of pictures is a good reward.

The Bad:

Once your child has mastered all five levels, there aren't additional pictures to solve. The developer indicates within the app that more levels will be coming with newer versions, which will be very beneficial to this app.

For children who aren't as good at spatial reasoning they could quickly become frustrated and not have the patience to try and complete the pictures. Parents also need to make sure that their child is old enough for this app since small children won't be able to be as successful at it as older children.

Additional:

"Pictorial" is creative, unique, fun and challenging—all the elements both kids and parents want in an app. The complexity of the animation with rotating the stars to form pictures is impressive, and kids will spend a lot of time trying to solve the constellations and complete each level. It's definitely a win for everyone!

Telling Time - Photo Touch Game

Recommended Age Group: Kindergarten-Elementary

Grades:

- Educational--B

- Fun—B

- Overall—B

Price: $0.99 (No free version)

Developer: GrasshopperApps.com

Compatible: iPhone

Review

What it is:

Help your child learn how to tell time on an analog clock with "Telling Time - Photo Touch Game." This is an easy-to-use app that kids will enjoy and learn how to read a clock using sight, sound and touch.

How it Works:

Select "Play" and the app starts. A screen appears with three or more analog clocks each telling a different time using hour and minute hands. A voiceover says a time. Touch the clock that shows that time. If it's correct, the voiceover provides positive such as "well done" or "awesome!"

One question is asked per screen. After a correct answer, the voiceover asks a different question with the new clocks showing different times. After three correct answers, the app adds a fourth clock, increasing the level of difficulty.

There are a number of customizable options on the settings menu. Parents can select sounds, hints, voiceover reinforcements, and the number of clocks to appear on the screen (between three and ten). A key settings option is to have all the correct answers as clocks with a specific time. And, these times can be positioned at any five-minute increment. For example, clocks can be set at "five past twelve" or "eight twenty-five."

There is also an option to personalize the app by recording different voices or uploading photos of clocks around the house so children can practice with what is familiar to them.

What it Teaches/Develops:

This app teaches kids how to tell time using hour and minute hands. They can learn a variety of lessons, including time by full hour and half-past hours, and each clock is in five-minute increments.

The Good:

This app is very easy to navigate and the concept is simple. The graphics are clear and the voiceover is easy to understand. The customizable options are good so that parents can adjust the activity according to their child's skill level and focus on the aspects of time they need to practice.

The Bad:

This app only applies to children who do not yet know how to tell time. Older elementary school children will not need this app.

Additional:

"Telling Time - Photo Touch Game" is a simple but effective way to teach children how to tell time. It's a good resource that parents can use at home to reinforce what kids are learning at school, as well as serve as an educational tool for home-schooled children.

Bonus: Educational Tools for all ages

Using videos to educate kids.

Recommended Age Group: All ages

Grades:

- Educational—B+

- Fun—A+

- Overall—A-

Price: Free (No paid version)

Developer: PBS Kids

Compatible: iPhone

Review

What it is:

Kids can watch their favorite PBS shows wherever you go with "PBS KIDS Video." This free app has shows from all of the popular PBS series, including "Curious George," "The Cat in the Hat Knows a Lot About That," "Dinosaur Train, "Super Why!" "Sesame Street" and "Wild Kratts."

How it Works:

The main menu has a scrolling list of all the popular children's PBS TV shows. The middle of the screen shows rotating ads for each series. Click on any of the icons in the scrolling menu to select a show from that series. The 30 minute clip will play on the full screen just like a regular TV show. Tap the screen at any time to return to the main menu.

There is a parental menu as well. From here parents can find local PBS stations and show times as well as read information about each TV series. There are more than 1,000 videos available from the 12 different shows mentioned above. Any of the episodes can be added to your child's favorites menu for easy viewing.

What it Teaches/Develops:

This is a very entertaining app for kids. It essentially turns the iPad into a portable

TV so that kids can watch their favorite educational PBS shows anywhere they go.

The Good:

The TV shows come across clear and vibrant on the iPad's screen. It truly is just like watching TV from home. All of the shows are the same quality programming that is available on PBS. Parents can decide which shows to let kids watch and for how long to watch them. It's a good way to monitor how much and what kind of TV shows kids are exposed to.

The Bad:

There is nothing negative about this app.

Additional:

This is a great free app parents can download and know they have a quality, short TV program for their kids to watch when they're on the go. They are commercial free and there isn't access to any videos other than the children's PBS shows.

iTubeList - YouTube Playlist Finder (with kids video collection)

Recommended Age Group: All ages

Grades:

- Educational--B

- Fun—A

- Overall—B+

Price: Free (Continuous play option in-app for $0.99)

Developer: GO2STAT LLC

Compatible: iPhone

Review

What it is:

YouTube is one of the most popular sites on the Internet, and now kids can watch their favorite YouTube videos right on the iPad with "iTubeList - YouTube Playlist Finder." This app gives parents access to a Kids Video Collection of more than 90 videos and lets them easily create a YouTube playlist of their own that is suitable for their children.

How it Works:

There are two ways to create playlists:

1. Access the Kids Video Collection already provided in the app. The Kids Video Collection consists of more than 90 videos that are grouped into five categories: Cartoons, Disney, Fun songs, Kids Learning and Nursery Rhymes.

To access The Kids Video Collection, select the "+" symbol on the top of the home page, then select "Kids Video Collection," and choose from one of five categories. A list of YouTube videos appears. Touch the "+" symbol and all the episodes in this category are instantly added to the playlist.

2. Create a custom playlist of YouTube videos. Adding videos from a personal YouTube account, Channel and/or a Playlist ID, does this. There is also the option to search using keywords for YouTube videos on the app's home page. When kids launch the app, they will be able to pick and choose from the playlist simply by touching the screen.

What it Teaches/Develops:

Parents can use this app for a variety of activities, whether it's to download educational videos, a child's favorite TV show or even music. Parents control the content so their children have access to age appropriate YouTube videos.

The Good:

This app is an excellent way for parents to control the videos children are exposed to on YouTube. The app is easy to use and works seamlessly with YouTube. A fast way to start is by exploring the Kids Video Collection that includes fourteen educational videos.

The Bad:

Ads do appear when playing YouTube videos in the app. The $0.99 version of the app eliminates the ads. The upgrade also allows for continuous video playing.

Additional:

This is the app parents need to consider since it allows their kids to have exposure to the YouTube site without the risk of viewing inappropriate content. It's a definite win for both parents and kids.

Apps For Kids Reviews

If you would like to receive free reviews of top iPad apps for kids that are educational and fun, please contact me at: appsforkidsreviews@gmail.com.

www.ingramcontent.com/pod-product-compliance
Lightning Source LLC
Chambersburg PA
CBHW071155050326
40689CB00011B/2116